W9-CLL-438

THE GREENHAVEN PRESS COMPANION TO
Literary Movements and Genres

Satire

Laura K. Egendorf, *Book Editor*

Daniel Leone, *President*

Bonnie Szumski, *Publisher*

Scott Barbour, *Managing Editor*

David M. Haugen, *Series Editor*

GREENHAVEN PRESS
SAN DIEGO, CALIFORNIA

GALE GROUP
TM
THOMSON LEARNING

Detroit • New York • San Diego • San Francisco
Boston • New Haven, Conn. • Waterville, Maine
London • Munich

Every effort has been made to trace the owners of copy-
righted material. The articles in this volume may have
been edited for content, length, and/or reading level. The
titles have been changed to enhance the editorial purpose.
Those interested in locating the original source will find
the complete citation on the first page of each article.

Library of Congress Cataloging-in-Publication Data

Satire / Laura K. Egendorf, book editor.
        p. cm. — (The Greenhaven Press companion to
literary movements and genres)
    Includes bibliographical references and index.
    ISBN 0-7377-1089-6 (pbk. : alk. paper) —
ISBN 0-7377-1090-X (lib. : alk. paper)
    1. Satire—History and criticism. I. Egendorf, Laura K.,
1973– . II. Series.

PN6149.S2 S27   2002
809.7—dc21   2001040865
                                                CIP

Cover photo: Art Resource, NY
Library of Congress: 13, 17, 93
North Wind Picture Archives: 86, 105

Copyright © 2002 by Greenhaven Press,
an imprint of The Gale Group
10911 Technology Place
San Diego, CA 92127
Printed in the U.S.A.

CONTENTS

Chapter 1: The Elements of Satire

1. Satire as a Form of Humor
by Gilbert Highet

Satire borrows several elements from other forms of humor. The genre's use of farce and abusive language to make its readers recognize their errors places it between the poles of comedy and invective.

2. The Role of Irony in Satire *by Alvin B. Kernan*

Irony is the satirist's strongest weapon. By using irony, satirists are able to depict the true character of their targets and the foolishness of their pretensions.

3. Invective in Satire *by David Worcester*

Although anger is common to satire, satirists express their invective through indirect methods. These methods, which include epithets and similes, make the writers' views more appealing to their readers.

4. Religion as a Target of Satire
by Edward A. Bloom and Lillian D. Bloom

Religious satire aims to expose hypocrisy and paradoxes in an attempt to make people question their beliefs. Although these satires vary in tone, their ultimate goal is not a harsh denunciation of beliefs but a humbling of those who unquestioningly assume a faith and piety that is inconsistent with the reality of being human.

5. Satire and Politics *by Leonard Feinberg*

The political views of satirists range from radical to conservative and can change as they age. Political satire tends to attack views with which the satirists disagree, instead of presenting support for the satirists' own beliefs.

6. The Treatment of Women in Satire
by Matthew Hodgart

Women are a common target in satire. Some satirists portray women as lascivious and disgusting, while others acknowledge the power women hold over men.

Chapter 2: Classic Satire

Chapter 3: Modern Satire

Chapter 4: Responding to Satire

FOREWORD

The study of literature most often involves focusing on an individual work and uncovering its themes, stylistic conventions, and historical relevance. It is also enlightening to examine multiple works by a single author, identifying similarities and differences among texts and tracing the author's development as an artist.

While the study of individual works and authors is instructive, however, examining groups of authors who shared certain cultural or historical experiences adds a further richness to the study of literature. By focusing on literary movements and genres, readers gain a greater appreciation of influence of historical events and social circumstances on the development of particular literary forms and themes. For example, in the early twentieth century, rapid technological and industrial advances, mass urban migration, World War I, and other events contributed to the emergence of a movement known as American modernism. The dramatic social changes, and the uncertainty they created, were reflected in an increased use of free verse in poetry, the stream-of-consciousness technique in fiction, and a general sense of historical discontinuity and crisis of faith in most of the literature of the era. By focusing on these commonalities, readers attain a more comprehensive picture of the complex interplay of social, economic, political, aesthetic, and philosophical forces and ideas that create the tenor of any era. In the nineteenth-century American romanticism movement, for example, authors shared many ideas concerning the preeminence of the self-reliant individual, the infusion of nature with spiritual significance, and the potential of persons to achieve transcendence via communion with nature. However, despite their commonalities, American romantics often differed significantly in their thematic and stylistic approaches. Walt Whitman celebrated the communal nature of America's open democratic society, while Ralph Waldo

Emerson expressed the need for individuals to pursue their own fulfillment regardless of their fellow citizens. Herman Melville wrote novels in a largely naturalistic style whereas Nathaniel Hawthorne's novels were gothic and allegorical.

Another valuable reason to investigate literary movements and genres lies in their potential to clarify the process of literary evolution. By examining groups of authors, literary trends across time become evident. The reader learns, for instance, how English romanticism was transformed as it crossed the Atlantic to America. The poetry of Lord Byron, William Wordsworth, and John Keats celebrated the restorative potential of rural scenes. The American romantics, writing later in the century, shared their English counterparts' faith in nature; but American authors were more likely to present an ambiguous view of nature as a source of liberation as well as the dwelling place of personal demons. The whale in Melville's *Moby-Dick* and the forests in Hawthorne's novels and stories bear little resemblance to the benign pastoral scenes in Wordsworth's lyric poems.

Each volume in Greenhaven Press's Companions to Literary Movements and Genres series begins with an introductory essay that places the topic in a historical and literary context. The essays that follow are carefully chosen and edited for ease of comprehension. These essays are arranged into clearly defined chapters that are outlined in a concise annotated table of contents. Finally, a thorough chronology maps out crucial literary milestones of the movement or genre as well as significant social and historical events. Readers will benefit from the structure and coherence that these features lend to material that is often challenging. With Greenhaven's Literary Movements and Genres in hand, readers will be better able to comprehend and appreciate the major literary works and their impact on society.

SATIRE: AN OVERVIEW

Satire is perhaps the most universal and most specific of all literary genres. It is universal because targets for satire exist in almost every era and place: an unjust government, a hypocritical religious leader, a pretentious fellow writer. However, satire is very specific in that it cannot be adequately understood without understanding its context. To comprehend what the satirist is criticizing, the reader must grasp what was happening in politics, religion, literature, and society as a whole when the satire was written. Yet even as the context shifts and the specific targets change, the purpose of satire—to expose flaws, cruelty, and hypocrisy—has remained the same throughout history.

THE BEGINNINGS OF SATIRE

Satire has a lengthy history. In his book *The Art of Satire*, David Worcester observes, "All ancient literatures hint at the prevalence and dignity of satire in early times."[1] He cites early Irish and Arabic literature as among the first examples of satire. According to Matthew Hodgart in his book *Satire*, the genre was a part of even the most primitive cultures; premodern Eskimos, for example, sang songs of lampoon and derision.

The most sophisticated early satire was likely that of the ancient Greeks. Such writing includes the poetry of Archilocus, who allegedly once wrote invective so scathing that its target—Lycambes and his family—hanged themselves in shame. The first truly great Greek satirist, though, was the playwright Aristophanes, who lived in the fifth century B.C. When Aristophanes wrote his plays, Athens was facing Sparta in the Second Peloponnesian War. His satire *Lysistrata* concerns the desire of Athenian women to end the war and their effort to bring about peace by remaining celibate until the fighting ceased. He also argued for peace in *The Peace*. However, war was not Aristophanes' only target. He mocked the courts in *The Wasps* and the belief in communal property in *Ecclesiazusa*. And like the satirists who followed, Aristophanes aimed his pen at his contemporaries. Socrates was satirized in *The Clouds,* and the playwright Euripides was targeted in *The Frogs.*

Other important Greek satirists were Menippus, who satirized human foibles in the now-lost works "Necromancy" and "The Sale of Diogenes," and Lucian, who satirized superstitions and false philosophies. Lucian's satire *True History* contained fantastic elements such as trips to the moon and influenced later satirical works such as *Pantagruel* by François Rabelais and *Gulliver's Travels* by Jonathan Swift.

THE ROMAN SATIRISTS

Greek satire was followed by that of the Romans. The decadence of the Roman Empire inspired several satirists whose influences continued well into modern times. Gaius Lucilius, the first Roman satirist, authored thirty books of verse satires. Horace and Juvenal followed him. Horace, who wrote in the first century B.C., authored two books of satire on subjects such as avarice, and he penned two critiques of Lucilius. His satire, however, was primarily reflective and philosophical, not venomous.

In his *Sixteen Satires,* written between 98 and 128 A.D., Juvenal castigates much he does not like about Roman life, from promiscuous upper-class women to homosexuality to the behavior of the nouveau riche. His satire was much harsher than that written by Horace. Like many satirists, Juvenal was conservative; he protested not the status quo but newer and more radical ideas and behaviors that might pose a threat to his own lifestyle. This conservatism can be seen in Satire VI, on the subject of women, in which he laments changes in the behavior of women since the days of early Rome. Juvenal writes: "In the old days poverty/Kept Latin women chaste: hard work, too little sleep,/These were the things that saved their humble homes from corruption."[2] In his introduction to his translation of Juvenal's satires, Peter Green asserts:

> Juvenal writes from a very limited viewpoint, and the traverse of his attack is correspondingly narrow. Throughout his life, so far as we can tell, he never once questioned the social structure or the moral principles of the regime which had treated him so shabbily. . . . His approach to any social prob-

lem is, basically, one of static conservatism. . . . His most violent invective, whether borrowed from the common rhetorical stockpot or the fruit of his own obsessions, is reserved for those who, in one way or another, threaten to disrupt the existing pattern of society.[5]

MEDIEVAL AND RENAISSANCE SATIRE

Like much nonreligious art and literature, satire was neglected after the fall of the Roman Empire in the fifth century. However, by the twelfth century, satire was revived in England. According to Hugh Walker in *English Satire and Satirists*, religion became an increasingly popular target among monks and clergymen: "It is the feature of the satires of the time that the strictures on the Church are pronounced by men who are either themselves ecclesiastic or at least in sympathy with the institution which they criticise."[4] Monasteries were a particular mark of medieval satirists. The clerics Gerald of Wales and Walter Map penned satires that chastised what they saw as the profligate behavior—for example, overly lavish meals and sexual incontinence—of the larger monastic orders. Gerald and Map did not focus solely on monasteries; they also satirized the behavior of the English court. In an article on monastic satire, Edward Coleman points out the broadening scope of these works: "The criticism of monasteries by Gerald, Map and others at the end of the twelfth century may have reflected a widespread unease with certain aspects of Christian society."[5]

In the fourteenth century, satire in France took the form of fabliaux, short tales performed by minstrels that mock human weaknesses and disrespect authority. The fabliaux influenced many writers, including Englishman Geoffrey Chaucer. Chaucer's collection, *The Canterbury Tales*, includes six such tales. Written between 1387 and 1400, the *Tales* satirize religion in the stories told by the Friar, Pardoner, and Summoner, while the Wife of Bath's tale focuses on marriage and women. *The Canterbury Tales* demonstrate Chaucer's skillful use of irony, an important element in satire. Worcester writes: "[His] ironical manner controls the tone, keeps his reader alert and amused, and diffuses an air of genial skepticism and penetrating humor throughout his major writings."[6]

Two centuries after *The Canterbury Tales*, Elizabethans began to pen satires that were heavily influenced by Juvenal,

Horace, and other classical writers. Juvenal's impact can be seen in the invective and indignation of Elizabethan satirists such as Joseph Hall, whose works include the verse satire *Virgidemiarum Sex Libri*, which attacks poetry and astrology, and John Marston, whose satires include the poem *The Metamorphosis of Pigmalion's Image* and the verse satire *The Scourge of Villanie*. According to literary critic O.J. Campbell: "They worked themselves up into a state of vociferous indignation; their voices became strident and their lash played upon the prisoners of evil with cruel abandon."[7] However, this anger was not without a purpose; Elizabethan satirists were concerned with the economic and social abuses of their time, including oppression by landlords, corrupt religious leaders, and the hypocritical and debauched behavior of the English court. Ben Jonson also targeted fellow writers, in particular Marston and Thomas Dekker, in his satires *Cynthia's Revels* and *The Poetaster*. Juvenal influenced Jonson's play *Volpone*, which satirizes the corruption and immorality of England much as Juvenal castigates Rome.

Outside England, French writer François Rabelais and Spanish novelist Miguel de Cervantes were two of the major continental satirists of the sixteenth century. Rabelais's book *Gargantua and Pantagruel* is largely parody; his writing style imitates that of the Bible, as well as medical, legal, and theological works. Like many other satirists, Rabelais aims his ire at people he knows and does not respect. Although filled with fantasy lands populated by monsters, his book is really a vivid portrayal of then contemporary France. J.M. Cohen, in his introduction to his translation of the novel, writes: "Rabelais . . . gives us the whole of French life in the two decades before 1550. In his distorting mirror he shows them perhaps more accurately than a historian, for he sees them from the standpoint of a giant."[8]

Cervantes's *Don Quixote*, regarded as the first modern novel, is a satire of the chivalric romance. The title character is Alonso Quixano, a poor Spaniard in his fifties who spends much of his time reading those romances. He grows to believe that he is Don Quixote de la Mancha, a young and brave knight errant (a knight who seeks adventure) and pursues escapades with his equally unlikely page, Sancho Panza. E.C. Riley asserts that Cervantes has written a multi-layered parody: "Cervantes's originality lies not in parodying [chivalric novels] himself . . . , but in making the mad Knight parody them involuntarily in his efforts to bring them, by means of imitation, literally to life."[9]

SATIRE'S GREATEST ERA

Satire perhaps reached its peak in the eighteenth century in the works of Irish-English writer Jonathan Swift, English poet Alexander Pope, and French writer Voltaire. In his essay "Swift: The View from Within the Satire," Ernest Tuveson summarizes the commonly held view of the "Dean of Dublin": "Jonathan Swift, to his own age and for subsequent generations, became in the popular estimation 'The Satirist' almost as Shakespeare is established as 'The Dramatist.'"[10]

Three of Swift's most notable satires were "The Battle of the Books," *A Tale of a Tub*, and "A Modest Proposal." The first work, written in 1697, is Swift's take on the debate among late-seventeenth-century authors as to how their work compared with that of the ancient writers; Swift takes the side of the ancients. "Battle" includes Swift's famous definition of satire: "Satire is a sort of glass wherein beholders do generally discover everybody's face but their own."[11] Seven years later, he wrote *A Tale of a Tub*, an allegorical satire of contemporary religious quarrels.

In the late 1600s and early 1700s, Ireland was severely burdened by economic restrictions imposed by the British. Laws passed in 1665, 1680, and 1699 eliminated Ireland's ability to export cattle, dairy products, and woolens. Thirty years after the third law was passed, poverty and starvation remained serious problems in Ireland. In "A Modest Proposal"—perhaps the most understated title in literary history—Swift, or more precisely his treatise's narrator, offers a solution to Ireland's economic problems. Impoverished parents, the narrator opines, should sell their infants and small children as food to the wealthy. He declares that young children would make delicious and nutritious meals and notes wryly, "I grant this food will be somewhat dear, and therefore very proper for landlords, who, as they have already devoured most of the parents, seem to have the best title to the children."[12] Nearly three hundred years after its publication, "A Modest Proposal" remains one of the most scathing and shocking satires ever written.

Swift's most famous work is probably his novel *Gulliver's Travels*. On one level, the book parodies the popular travelogues of Swift's day. But the book is much more than a clever parody of other genres. The first part revolves around Lemuel Gulliver's voyage to Lilliput, a land of tiny people whose squabbles serve as political satire. Swift tackles the issues of war and government in Brobdingnag, a nation of giants whose king is repulsed by Gulliver's description of gunpowder and cannons. Gulliver's third voyage satirizes mathematicians and scientists. He lands in Laputa, whose residents are skilled in mathematics and music but who perform useless and impractical experiments and lack imagination. The final trip finds Gulliver in a country where the horses—known as Houyhnhnms—are peaceful and rational

Gulliver waves good-bye to the people of Lilliput.

and served by the Yahoos, a class of particularly repugnant humans. Gulliver's stay affects him so greatly that when he returns to England at the end of the novel, he is repulsed by the "Yahoos," including his own wife and children, who surround him. Gulliver's travels lead him to discover that he is an outsider who can no longer relate to his countrymen and is happier conversing with his horses than socializing with his family. The novel thus ends on a dark note, or what John Marshall Bullitt considers "a terrifying insight into evil . . . [that] is accompanied by all the bitterness of a profound disillusionment."[13]

Alexander Pope's works included the *Dunciad,* a satire of literary hacks, and *Imitations of Horace,* which targets social and political corruption. One of his most famed satires is the mock-epic poem "The Rape of the Lock." In this five-canto poem, which parodies the *Iliad, Paradise Lost,* and other epics, Pope describes events after a lock of hair is snipped from a young lady's head and in doing so, ridicules the fashionable society of early-eighteenth-century London. His parody includes elements common to epic poetry, such as a battle—which in "The Rape of the Lock" is a card game—and an appeal to the Muse. The language he uses is deliberately grander than the subject matter requires, as can be seen in the couplets in which the fair Belinda's hair is cut: "Fate urged the shears, and cut the sylph in twain,/(But airy substance soon unites again)/The meeting points the sacred hair dissever/From the fair head, for ever, and for ever!"[14]

While Swift and Pope were authoring important works of British satire, the Frenchman Voltaire was writing the novel *Candide*, the story of the young Candide; his teacher Pangloss; Candide's beloved Cunegonde; and the memorable characters Candide encounters in his travels. Voltaire's satire cuts a wide swath, targeting unrealistic seventeenth-century French novels in the absurd adventures of Candide—shipwrecks, earthquakes, frequent separations from and reunions with Cunegonde—as well as religious hypocrisy and greed and other human failings. He also targets the philosophy of Gottfried Wilhelm Leibniz, in particular Leibniz's theory that God created the best of all possible worlds. In his introduction to *Candide*, Daniel Gordon suggests that Voltaire "ridicules Leibniz's cosmic optimism"[15] through Pangloss, who repeatedly contends that all the disasters and evils that befall the travelers are for the greater good.

SATIRE AND PARODY IN AUSTEN AND BYRON

Although it may appear that historically the confrontational nature of satire is the exclusive province of men, women writers have certainly advanced the genre, perhaps most significantly nineteenth-century English author Jane Austen. Unlike her male peers, Austen did not satirize political situations. However, religion was a target of her novels. Austen was the daughter and sister of clergymen and did pen several positive portrayals of that profession. That did not prevent her from creating characters such as the fawning and doltish Mr. Collins (of *Pride and Prejudice*) and the snobbish Mr. Elton (of *Emma*). She also satirized the snobbery of the upper-middle and upper classes. She skewers the pretensions of women like Caroline Bingley in *Pride and Prejudice*—a woman who conveniently forgets that her wealth comes from the fortune her father developed in trade, and looks down upon those whose relatives must work for a living.

Of Austen's six novels, the most purely satirical is *Northanger Abbey*. Though it was not published until after her death in 1817, Austen began writing the novel in the 1790s, when the Gothic novel and the sentimental novel enjoyed popularity. Through the plot of *Northanger Abbey* and the portrayal of the heroine, Catherine Morland, Austen satirizes both genres. Gothic novels, popularized by authors such as Horace Walpole and Ann Radcliffe, typically featured elements such as dark and forboding abbeys and heroines in perennial danger. *Northanger Abbey* mocks the conventions of Gothic novels by making the title home a well-lit and modern residence and by featuring a scene in which Catherine becomes unnecessarily frightened by the contents of a bedroom chest. Sentimental novels centered on the romantic adventures of impossibly beautiful and talented heroines. Austen makes it clear that Catherine is far from a traditional heroine: "She had a thin awkward figure, a sallow skin without colour, dark lank hair, and strong features; . . . She never could learn or understand anything before she was taught; and sometimes not even then, for she was often inattentive, and occasionally stupid."[16]

Another preeminent satirist of the early nineteenth century was Lord Byron. Despite being grouped among them, George Gordon Byron frequently satirized Romantic poets. In 1809, two years after his volume *Hours of Idleness* garnered a negative reaction in the *Edinburgh Review*, Byron responded with the poem "English Bards and Scotch Reviewers," which pilloried the reviewer and nearly all the members of the Romantic school. Byron's negative opinion of most of his peers is again evident in the epic poem *Don Juan*. In the prologue he ridicules fellow poets Robert Southey, Samuel Taylor Coleridge, and William Wordsworth:

> You—Gentlemen! by dint of long seclusion
> From better company, have kept your own
> At Keswick, and, through still continued fusion
> Of one another's minds, at last have grown
> To deem as a most logical conclusion,
> That Poesy has wreaths for you alone:
> There is narrowness in such a notion,
> Which makes me wish you'd change your lakes for Ocean.[17]

However, Romantic poets are not the only victims in Byron's satires. Byron also targets his former wife, Annabella Milbanke, through the character of Donna Inez, the mother of Don Juan. Like Lady Byron, Donna Inez is skilled in mathematics and has an excellent memory. In addition, Byron mocks his wife's prudishness. *Don Juan* as a whole displays Byron's distaste for convention, hypocrisy, intolerance, and restrictions on freedom. Byron's love of liberty—

which would indirectly bring about his death by a fever contracted when he helped the Greeks in their revolt against the Turks—included a criticism of the British government's domestic policies, including the repression of uprisings by the English poor. Claude Moore Fuess, in *Lord Byron as a Satirist in Verse*, summarizes the purpose of Byron's writings: "Since Byron was a radical and a rebel, his satire was devoted, so far as it concerned itself with political questions, to the glorification of liberty in all its forms."[18]

Numerous literary styles influenced *Don Juan*, including Italian epic poetry, Gothic romance, and mock-heroic poems. Juvenal's influence also shows strongly. Like the classic satirist, Byron uses invective and emphasizes the role of fate. Byron's depiction of Don Juan's sexual encounters, in particular Juan's dalliance with Gulbeyaz, also bears witness to Juvenal's continual importance to satirists. Along with these homages, Byron parodies the Ten Commandments and other parts of the Bible.

THE DEVELOPMENT OF AMERICAN SATIRE

While satire was flourishing in England, it began to gain a foothold in the former colonies. American satire tended toward political rather than religious targets and also lacked the irony common to its English counterparts. As would be expected, much of American satire praised democracy and castigated monarchies. However, Lewis P. Simpson notes that not all American satirists were convinced of democracy's advantages. In his essay "The Satiric Mode: The Early National Wits," Simpson writes, "When we turn to satires predicated on overtly reactionary views of democratic developments in America . . . we find uncomplicated visions of present disorder and impending catastrophe."[19] One example of these doomsday satires is Lemuel Hopkins's mock-epic poem *The Anarchiad*. Hugh Henry Brackenridge's novel *Modern Chivalry*, written between 1792 and 1805, also pokes fun at the follies and mistakes of the young democracy.

Better-known American writers also wrote satire, including Washington Irving, whose *Knickerbockers' History of New York* chiefly targeted the early Dutch settlers, and James Fenimore Cooper, who satirizes Puritans in *The Wept of Wish-ton-Wish* and America's values, provincialism, and greed in *Home as Found*. Nathaniel Hawthorne ridicules the Brook Farm experiment—a six-year attempt at communal living with which Hawthorne, Ralph Waldo Emerson, Margaret Fuller, and other religious and literary leaders had been associated—in *The Blithedale Romance.*

Although not exclusively a satirist, Mark Twain wrote several works that criticized both contemporary American mores and traditional European values. *A Connecticut Yankee in King Arthur's Court* exposes the hypocrisy and barbarism of Arthurian England, as well as what Twain sees as a despotic Catholic Church, while at the same time criticizing Americans' nostalgia for chivalry and other archaic ideals. *The Prince and the Pauper* and *Joan of Arc* target the government and church-supported barbarism and greed found in sixteenth-century England and fifteenth-century France, respectively.

Mark Twain

Despite the criticism of Americans in *A Connecticut Yankee,* Twain is largely proud of his society. According to Frank Baldanza in *Mark Twain: An Introduction and Interpretation:* "[There] lurks beneath the surface of all three books the assumption that late nineteenth-century American democracy has remedied most of these ills and that it is the ideal norm against which to measure the failure of other civilizations."[20]

Nonetheless, Twain is not always so forgiving of his fellow citizens. *The Gilded Age,* cowritten with Charles Dudley Warner, satirizes the corruption of President Ulysses S. Grant's administration. *Innocents Abroad* mocks the behavior of American tourists in Europe.

MODERN SATIRE

Because Twain was not primarily a satirist, the title of greatest American satirist may go to Sinclair Lewis. According to Frederick J. Hoffman, "Sinclair Lewis assumed every possible role with respect to the middle class. He was its critic and judge, its satirist and parodist, minister to its victims, Balzacian commentator upon its many-sided life, and 'liberal' guardian of its political activities."[21] Between 1920 and 1929, Lewis released five of the most famous modern satires: *Main*

Street, Babbitt, Arrowsmith, Elmer Gantry, and *Dodsworth.* In the first two novels, Lewis targets small-town life through the characters of Carol Kennicott, who seeks to impose her romantic values on Gopher Prairie, and George Babbitt, a successful but small-minded realtor in Zenith. *Arrowsmith* details the experiences of doctor Martin Arrowsmith, while *Elmer Gantry* tells the tale of a hypocritical and lecherous preacher, and *Dodsworth* revolves around the behavior of a wealthy American couple. Each of these novels castigated the values of middle America. In his essay "Lewis's Satire—A Negative Emphasis," Daniel R. Brown writes: "Most of Lewis's assaults were upon standardization, religious provinciality, narrow-mindedness, and hypocrisy."[22] These attacks were often angry, reflecting the influence of Juvenal. However, Lewis is not always consistent; in some works, he criticizes liberalism, in others he praises it.

Many important satires were written in the two decades following Lewis's masterworks. Only three years after *Dodsworth,* Aldous Huxley released *Brave New World.* Unlike Lewis, whose novels focused on contemporary life, Huxley set his satire in the future. *Brave New World* is the story of a dystopia—a utopia gone horribly wrong. The novel presents a world in which babies are propagated in test tubes and no one questions the society's rigid caste system. The characters that question these norms, particularly the character of the Savage, become castoffs. The Savage has grown up on a reservation outside the "brave new world," the result of a traditional pregnancy. Unlike most of the people he encounters, the Savage wants to experience the gamut of emotions and experiences: "I don't want comfort. I want God, I want poetry, I want real danger, I want freedom, I want goodness. I want sin."[23] Ultimately the Savage cannot survive in this world where emotion is stifled and thwarted through drugs and promiscuity, and so he hangs himself in resignation but also martyrdom for a lost cause.

In *Brave New World,* Huxley targets traditional utopias, such as H.G. Wells's *The First Men in the Moon* and Sir Francis Bacon's *New Atlantis,* and the way in which science affects modern society. Jerome Meckler, author of *Aldous Huxley: Satire and Structure,* observes:

> One of the chief reasons why Huxley wrote the novel, it is tempting to conclude, was to discredit, if not discourage, the sort of utopian writing he was familiar with. The urge to

write a literary satire on existing works went hand in hand with the desire to challenge, by means of a correcting, less optimistic vision of his own, the picture of the future that science was enthusiastically offering.[24]

British author George Orwell also used dystopias as satirical settings. His two most famous satires, *Animal Farm* and *Nineteen Eighty-Four*, are dark tales of societies in which individuality has been destroyed. *Animal Farm* is a satirical allegory about farm animals that overthrow their owners and establish control of the farm. The pigs, horses, dogs, and other animals represent important figures in the Russian Revolution and the ensuing regime of Joseph Stalin. At first, the animals agree to treat each other as equals, but gradually the pig Napoleon—the Stalin character—takes control. Napoleon has his rivals killed or driven off Animal Farm and by the end of the novel, he and the remaining pigs are indistinguishable from the humans they replaced. However, *Animal Farm* is more than just a political satire. Stephen Jay Greenblatt observes: "[The] book's major concern is not with [historical] incidents but with the essential horror of the human condition. There have been, are, and always will be pigs in every society, Orwell states, and they will always grab power."[25]

Like *Brave New World*, *Nineteen Eighty-Four* involves the tragedy of a man who tries to live outside the strict rules of society. In this case, the man is Winston Smith, who lives in Oceania, a miserable and impoverished society where privacy and free speech do not exist. Smith's brief attempt at rebellion ends with brainwashing and torture that compel Smith to accept the rules under which he lives and his likely imminent death. Orwell's satire is cleverly encoded even in his ironic use of language. In the language spoken in Oceania, almost every word signifies its opposite; the Ministry of Peace encourages war, while the Ministry of Truth revises and falsifies history.

Another prominent satirist in the last century is Nathanael West, who penned *Miss Lonelyhearts* and *The Day of the Locust* in the 1930s. The former book is about a spiritually desolate advice columnist and the people he encounters; the latter is centered on Tod Hackett, a young artist living in Hollywood. Both novels satirize the shallowness of modern culture and its obsession with violence and sexuality. The threads of West's satire culminate in the final scene of *The*

Day of the Locust, in which a crowd riots at a movie premiere.

Two of the more noteworthy satirists of the latter half of the twentieth century are Joseph Heller and Kurt Vonnegut. Heller's *Catch-22* is a scathing satire of World War II and the military bureaucracy that drives soldiers mad. Unlike his counterparts Winston Smith and the Savage, Heller's protagonist John Yossarian is able to rebel against the system and successfully escape. In works such as *Cat's Cradle* and *Slaughterhouse-Five*, Kurt Vonnegut uses a satirical form of science fiction in order to offer his views on World War II (in particular the bombing of Dresden, which Vonnegut lived through as a prisoner of war), science, and philosophy.

SATIRE IN TODAY'S WORLD

Although contemporary writers continue to create booklength satire, including Vonnegut and political satirist P.J. O'Rourke (whose *All the Trouble in the World* can be considered a 1990s version of *Innocents Abroad*), satire has taken newer forms in recent decades. Satire is more likely to be found in periodicals, including the *Onion* and the now-defunct *Spy* and *Might*, and in films: Stanley Kubrick's *Dr. Strangelove* satirizes the cold war, while Rob Reiner's *This Is Spinal Tap* parodies heavy metal's music and lifestyle. Even television shows such as *The Simpsons* and the monologues and sketches found on late-night variety and talk shows continue to target popular culture and political icons.

However, satire is no longer as prevalent as in centuries past. It is not for lack of subjects; the flaws and hypocrisies of American politicians and British royalty could readily fill several volumes. Rather, satire has lost a considerable amount of its power because it is no longer seen as a threat. Satirists once faced severe censorship as far back as ancient Rome, when the emperor Augustus passed a law imposing the death penalty on the writers of satires and lampoons. In 1599 an edict was passed in England that forbade the publication of satire. Censorship was likewise strong when Swift and Pope wrote. Progovernment writers sought to restrict political satire in 1720s England. In 1737, the Stage Licensing Act was used to limit satire in British plays. Today, however, satirists write without fear.

In his analysis of the genre, *Introduction to Satire*, Leonard Feinberg offers several other reasons why satire has lost some of its popularity. He contends that to many potential readers, satire is too uncomfortable, negative, and disillusioning. Unlike other genres, *"satire provides neither the catharsis of tragedy [nor] the escapism of romantic literature. The effect of satire is ambivalent and ambiguous. It arouses conflicting emotions but does not quite satisfy them."*[26]

Satire may be less popular in modern society, but the lessons it has taught throughout its history remain important. While Feinberg maintains that satire lacks a large present-day audience, he also observes that the genre still serves an important purpose. As Feinberg explains: "By reading satire, one can see the ubiquity of social problems and the continuity of social criticism. . . . He will be constantly reminded that the conventional picture of the world is, to varying degrees, a false picture."[27]

NOTES

1. David Worcester, *The Art of Satire*. New York: Russell and Russell, 1960, p. 148.

2. Peter Green, trans., Juvenal, *The Sixteen Satires*. London: Penguin, 1974, p. 137.

3. Green, *The Sixteen Satires*, p. 23.

4. Hugh Walker, *English Satire and Satirists*. New York: Dutton, 1925, p. 2.

5. Edward Coleman, "Nasty Habits—Satire and the Medieval Monk," *History Today*, June 1993, p. 35.

6. Worcester, *The Art of Satire*, p. 101.

7. O.J. Campbell, *Comicall Satyre and Shakespeare's "Troilus and Cresida."* San Marino, CA: Adcraft Press, 1938, p. 35.

8. J.M. Cohen, trans., François Rabelais, *Gargantua and Pantagruel*. London: Penguin, 1955, p. 21.

9. E.C. Riley, "Literature and Life in *Don Quixote*," reprinted in Lowry Nelson Jr., ed., *Cervantes: A Collection of Critical Essays*. Englewood Cliffs, NJ: Prentice-Hall, 1969, p. 124.

10. Ernest Tuveson, "Swift: The View from Within the Satire," in H. James Jensen and Malvin R. Zirker Jr., eds., *The Satirist's Art*. Bloomington: Indiana University Press, 1972, p. 55.

11. Jonathan Swift, "The Battle of the Books," in Jonathan Swift, *A Modest Proposal and Other Satirical Works*. New York: Dover, 1996, p. 2.

12. Jonathan Swift, "A Modest Proposal," in Swift, *A Modest Proposal and Other Satirical Works*, p. 54.

13. John Marshall Bullitt, *Jonathan Swift and the Anatomy of Satire: A Study of Satiric Technique*. Cambridge, MA: Harvard University Press, 1953, p. 65.

14. Alexander Pope, "The Rape of the Lock," Canto 3, lines 152–55. John R. Clark and Anna Motto, eds., *Satire—That Blasted Art*. New York: Putnam, 1973, p. 159.

15. Daniel Gordon, trans. and ed., Voltaire, *Candide*. Boston: Bedford/St. Martin's, 1999, p. 21.

16. Jane Austen, *Northanger Abbey*. Ware, England: Wordsworth Classics, 1993, p. 3.

17. Lord Byron, *Don Juan*, Dedication, stanza 5. Boston: Houghton Mifflin, 1958, p. 7.

18. Claude Moore Fuess, *Lord Byron as a Satirist in Verse*. New York: Russell and Russell, 1964, p. 215.

19. Lewis P. Simpson, "The Satiric Mode: The Early National Wits," in Louis D. Rubin Jr., ed., *The Comic Imagination in American Literature*. New Brunswick, NJ: Rutgers University Press, 1973, p. 55.

20. Frank Baldanza, *Mark Twain: An Introduction and Interpretation*. New York: Holt, Rinehart, and Winston, 1961, p. 70.

21. Frederick J. Hoffman, "Critique of the Middle Class: Sinclair Lewis's *Babbitt*," reprinted in *The Merrill Studies in Babbitt*. Columbus, OH: Charles E. Merrill, 1971, p. 45.

22. Daniel R. Brown, "Lewis's Satire—A Negative Emphasis," in *Renascence*, Winter 1966, p. 63.

23. Aldous Huxley, *Brave New World*. New York: Harper and Row, 1932, p. 163.

24. Jerome Meckler, *Aldous Huxley: Satire and Structure*. New York: Barnes and Noble, 1969, p. 177.

25. Stephen Jay Greenblatt, *Three Modern Satirists: Waugh, Orwell, and Huxley*. New Haven, CT: Yale University Press, 1965, p. 65.

26. Leonard Feinberg, *Introduction to Satire*. Ames: Iowa State University Press, 1967, p. 272.

27. Feinberg, *Introduction to Satire*, p. 274.

CHAPTER 1

The Elements of Satire

Satire as a Form of Humor

Gilbert Highet

In the following selection, Gilbert Highet explains
how satire borrows elements from other forms of humor such as invective, lampoon, comedy, and farce.
Writers of invective and lampoon use abusive language to shame and humiliate their targets, while
comedic and farcical writers wish to evoke laughter.
According to Highet, although satire is more similar to
invective, for the most part it falls between those two
poles of humor because its purpose is to use laughter
and invective to make its readers recognize and correct their follies. Highet, who died in 1978, was a professor at Columbia University. He was also the author
of more than twenty books, including *The Classical
Tradition: Greek and Roman Influences on Western Literature, Juvenal the Satirist,* and *The Anatomy of
Satire,* the source of the following viewpoint.

Satire can be mistaken for other forms of art and literature,
unless its emotional and moral effects are clearly defined
and understood. Aesthetic types are not walled off from one
another by impenetrable barriers. At their extremes they di-
verge clearly and unmistakably; but they spring from roots
which lie near to one another in the human soul; and,
through much of their development, they grow closely together, so that only the boldest and most determined representative of each type appears to define that particular type,
while others keep crossing frontiers and mingling powers
and competing with one another, just as do people, and lan-
guages, and societies. Certain forms of literature are particularly close kinsmen and near neighbors of satire, and often
exchange with it both costumes and ideas.

INVECTIVE AND LAMPOON

On one side of satire lies its grim gruff old ancestor born in the stone caves, still echoing the martial monotony of the savages' skin drums roaring for the destruction of an enemy tribe, still shrieking with the furious passion of the witch-doctor denouncing a rival. This is Invective, whose parent on one side was anthropoid, and on the other, lupine. Lurking nearby is the smaller, weaker, but sometimes more dangerous mutant of Invective: a by-blow born of a snake and a toad, a hideous little creature with a mouth full of poisoned fangs. This is Lampoon, a parasite which has no life of its own and can exist only through destroying its victim.

Usually the lampoon is a poisoned dart, or a shower of filth, discharged with impunity on a helpless victim by his enemy. But sometimes the victim replies with another rain of garbage and venom; and the exchange grows into a regular duel. Each of the duellists endeavors to outshout, out-curse, and silence his opponent, whether by the appalling violence of his abuse, or by its piercing aptness, or by its passionate volubility, or by the unanswerable cleverness with which it is shaped and delivered. Word-duels of this type exist in many cultures, although they seldom emerge into the higher air of fine art and literature. Song-combats (called "drum matches") are recognized methods of settling disputes among the Eskimos of Greenland. Contemporary American Negroes have an institution called "the Dozens," in which rivals sing competing songs of abuse before a crowd: "the one whose fury stultifies his verbal agility loses the contest, and a sure sign of being bested is to hit one's opponent"[according to John Dollard]. The hero of the much-loved Argentine poem, José Hernández' *Martín Fierro* (1872–1879), is a roving gaucho who is never without his long knife and his tuneful guitar and loves fighting with either of them. One long section near the end of the poem consists of a duel in song between Martín and a Negro, which very nearly turns into a duel with knives, to the death.

THE CHARACTERISTIC QUALITIES OF WORD DUELS

There is no generally accepted word for these exchanges of abuse. However, they are sometimes called "flyting," from the old Scots word for scolding. Normally, they have the following characteristic qualities:

(1) They are, or seem to be, improvised.

(2) They are in strongly rhythmical verse, often married to music.

(3) They are relentlessly personal and outrageously scurrilous.

(4) They are responsive, or amoebaean: that is, when A has uttered his stanza of derision and hate, B must follow him in the same rhythmical pattern. In a close duel, he must use the same sentence-structure and even the same imagery. The challenger therefore has the advantage of taking the initiative, but the responder has always the chance of outdoing him.

(5) They are held in public, before a crowd which derives a complex pleasure from them: admiration of the skill of the contenders, delighted shock at the public use of obscenity and the revelation of secrets, sadistic amusement at the cruel humiliation they inflict upon each other.

A History of "Flyting"

Reciprocal exchanges of abuse used to be a popular amusement in Greece and Rome: during the procession from Athens to Eleusis for the rites of Demeter; at weddings in Italy where "Fescennine verses" were sung; at parties and at vintage-festivals. The only real entertainment which Horace and his friends had during their journey to Brindisi was such a duel between two professional comics. (One of them was called Cicirrus, a dialect word for "cock"; and they really put on a verbal cock-fight.) It is likely that the improvised shows called *saturae*, popular in Rome before the importation of genuine comedy from Greece, had such turns in them.

In literature, the slanging-match between Cleon and the Sausage-Seller in Aristophanes' *Knights* is a typical "flyting," and so are most of the contests between opposing half-choruses in Aristophanic comedy. Not all readers of pastoral poetry realize that it has its coarse brutal side, and that the "singing matches" of shepherds in Theocritus and Virgil are sometimes competitions in obscenity and cruelty—although both poets add the charm of elegant expression and subtle imagery: see Theocritus' fifth and Virgil's third bucolic poem.

The fifteenth-century Scottish poet William Dunbar is best known for his "lament in sickness," with its sad refrain *Timor mortis conturbat me;* but when he was well he was full of vigor: he has left fourteen pages of lively abuse exchanged with a fellow-poet, *The Flyting of Dunbar and*

Kennedy. It ends with a shout of triumph, calling on Kennedy
to "yield and flee the field," and go to hell—

> Pickit, wickit, convickit Lamp Lollardorum,
> Defamyt, blamyt, schamyt Primas Paganorum.
> Out! out! I schout, apon that snowt that snevillis.
> Tale tellare, rebellare, induellar wyth the devillis,
> Spynk, sink with stynk ad Tertara Termagorum.

This flyting is not satire. It is not comedy. Yet it has something in common with both kinds of literature. It springs
from some of the same deep roots in primitive society, and
in the combative challenging spirit of mankind.

COMEDY AND FARCE

Close to satire on the other side we see, cavorting about and
wearing gay masks and putting on funny hats and using un-
respectable words and disrupting solemn ceremonies, two
other siblings. These are Comedy and Farce. If it wanted to,
Comedy could be satire; and in nearly every satire there are
some elements of Farce. The main difference is that these
two beings are kind. They may be silly; they may tickle the
observer, or pinprick him (without drawing more than a
drop of blood), or hit him with a blown-up bladder, but they
do not hurt. Except to the most solemn or sensitive of mor-
tals, they are inoffensive. Comedy always wishes to evoke
laughter, or at least a smile of pure enjoyment. Farce does
not care what it does provided that everybody collapses into
unreasoning merriment. Most of us ignore this side of art;
some of us even ignore this side of life; but the fact remains.
The ridiculous is built into human existence. Many of our
essential activities, some of our deepest emotions, and several aspects of our physical appearance, are ludicrous. The
disrespectful youngster who contrives comedy and the grin-
ning chimpanzee who explores farce both recognize this
fact. Out of it they create gaiety which, although temporary,
is wholesome; sometimes a joke which lasts; and now and
then, almost involuntarily, a work of art.

These, then, are the closest kin of satire: on one side, invective and lampoon; on the other, comedy and farce. Invective and lampoon are full of hatred, and wish only to destroy.
Comedy and farce are rich with liking, and want to preserve,
to appreciate, to enjoy. The man who writes an invective
would be delighted if, after delivering it, he were told that his
subject had been overwhelmed by shame and obloquy and

had retired into oblivion. The lampoonist would like his victims to die of a hideous disease, or (like the enemies of Hipponax) to hang themselves. The writer of comedy or farce would be saddened by any such news. He likes people, not in spite of their peculiarities, but because of them. He could not endure the notion that all the oddities might disappear, and leave the world to routine and to him. Invective and lampoon look from above and from behind: one is the prosecuting attorney, the other the assassin. Comedy and farce look askance and from below: one is the amused friend who loves his friend's absurdities; the other is the servant who likes his master but cannot keep from befooling and mimicking him. As for satire, the satirist always asserts that he would be happy if he heard his victim had, in tears and self-abasement, permanently reformed; but he would in fact be rather better pleased if the fellow were pelted with garbage and ridden out of town on a rail. Satire is the literary equivalent of a bucket of tar and a sack of feathers. The purpose of invective and lampoon is to destroy an enemy. The purpose of comedy and farce is to cause painless undestructive laughter at human weaknesses and incongruities. The purpose of satire is, through laughter and invective, to cure folly and to punish evil; but if it does not achieve this purpose, it is content to jeer at folly and to expose evil to bitter contempt.

The Role of Irony in Satire

Alvin B. Kernan

In the following selection, Alvin B. Kernan asserts
that irony is an important element of satire. According to Kernan, satirists have offered several reasons
for why irony appeals to them: It is more scathing
than serious writing, it is less likely than a direct attack to incite violent responses by its targets, and it
provides the writer with a norm against which folly
can be measured. However, Kernan contends that
the greatest benefit of irony is that its use allows
satirists to attack the true character of their targets
and, at the same time, reveal the layers of pretense
these targets have built up around themselves, exposing the sham of this fake, affected reality. Kernan
is a senior advisor in the humanities at the Andrew
W. Mellon Foundation and a former English professor at Yale and Princeton. In addition to *The Plot of
Satire*, the source of the following selection, his
books include *The Cankered Muse: Satire of the English Renaissance* and *Modern Satire*.

The claim has been made that all irony is satire. While this
is obviously not so, it is true that nearly all satire makes use
of irony—ranging from the broadness of sarcasm to the extreme understatement of litotes—to such a degree that it is
now very nearly impossible to think of satire without thinking of irony. The satirist never seems to attack directly but
always pretends not to be doing what in fact he is doing. He
praises what he loathes, speaks with enthusiasm of utopias
which he proves to be wastelands, creates pleasant little
tales about the beasts and never seems to notice that his animals are reductions of human beings, solemnly dresses his
contemporaries in epic robes far too large for them, and con-

fidently puts Achille's spear in hands which cannot hold it.
Many of the structural devices consistently used in satire are
large-scale ironic techniques: mock encomium, mock epic,
mock utopia, the beast fable, the adventures of the simple-
ton, and the wise fool.

Irony is capable of immense variation in the hands of poets, but for working purposes there is no need to define it
more precisely than the generally accepted meaning: a situation, spoken or dramatized, is ironic when what seems to
be and what is are in some way opposed. In modern critical
usage the term has been expanded to refer to situations in
which the two components of an ironic situation are not
what seems and what is, but rather two different and seemingly contradictory aspects of reality, both equally true.
Irony then blends into ambiguity, tension, paradox, and ambivalence. This expansion of the term grows out of the facts
of literature, for in tragedy and certain kinds of poetry, particularly the Metaphysical, the movement is from pure irony
into paradox, from a situation in which one term of a pair of
opposites seems true and the other false, to a situation
where both are true. Oedipus at the end of his play is at once
the greatest of men and the most miserable, Othello becomes both judge and criminal. In satire, however, the two
poles of irony are ordinarily kept separate.

THE APPEAL OF IRONY

But why should satirists be so fond of irony? Most answers
to this question have not moved beyond the undeniable remark of the consistently ironic Horace [in *Sermones*] that
"ridicule more often cuts deeper into important matters than
does seriousness." But this leaves the real questions unan-
swered: Why is irony, which is what changes the serious to
the ridiculous in satire, witty and amusing? What gives it its
cutting edge? Another explanation frequently offered by the
satirists themselves—and supported by Freud—is that it is
necessary to deal with vice in an indirect, ironic manner because a direct attack would invite physical reprisals from
dangerous enemies. This argument is itself often ironic, for
it convicts the satirist's enemies of being vicious brutes before he begins to expose them. But while Ben Jonson may
have "beat [John] Marston and took his pistol from him" for
representing him on the stage in an unfavorable way [in
Jonson's play *The Poetmaster*], and while [John] Dryden may

have been roughed up by Rochester's thugs in the Rose Alley Ambuscade,[1] satirists on the whole have fared little worse at the hands of their enemies than other types of poets. Besides, irony never really fools anyone, and it removes the sting from a deadly insult only if the victim is a witty man. A third, less common, explanation of the marriage of satire and irony is that this way of writing permits its user at once to state the ways of dullness and to provide the norm against which folly can be known and judged. This is one of the prime functions of irony in satire and a junction point of the morality and wit which Dryden made the two chief components of this kind of poetry. . . .

But the most immediate function of satiric irony is disclosed by one of the satirist's regular defenses against the standard charge that he attacks the unfortunate and helpless out of pure savagery. Pope puts it this way:

> Deformity becomes the object of ridicule when a man sets up for being handsome: and so must Dulness when he sets up for a Wit. They are not ridicul'd because Ridicule in itself is or ought to be a pleasure; but because it is just, to undeceive or vindicate the honest and unpretending part of mankind from imposition. . . . Accordingly we find that in all ages, all vain pretenders, were they ever so poor or ever so dull, have been constantly the topicks of the most candid Satyrists, from the Codrus of Juvenal to the Damon of Boileau.

(*The Dunciad,*
"A Letter to the Publisher,"
Twickenham Edition)

In other words, satire does not deal with the naturally dull and deformed, but with the pretense of these and other weaknesses to be what they are not. Plain villainy would seem to lie equally beyond the range of satire, which would concern itself only with the brute who seems to be the benefactor. Such pretenses need not be conscious, however; the fool who really believes that he is wise is as proper a subject of satire as the double-dealer. The pretense of virtue and lip service to morality are as necessary to satire as the dullness they express, and it is part of the satiric creed that the nature of man is such that you seldom find the failing without the pretense: *Plus les mœurs sont dépravés, plus les expressions*

---

1. John Dryden was brutally attacked by men hired by John Rochester, the second Earl of Rochester, after Dryden was suspected of helping John Sheffield, then the Earl of Mulgrave, write a passage in Sheffield's "Essay on Satire" that commented on Rochester's lack of wit.

deviennent mesurées; on croit regagner en langage ce qu'on a perdu en vertu. ["More of the manners are depraved, more of the expressions are becoming measured; one believes that (in order) to regain in language what one lost in virtue."] Irony is the perfect rhetorical device for catching the pretense which reveals itself as sham, since its two terms permit the poet to create both the pretense and the truth at once. He no longer need tell us, as the sermonist or reformer does, that men are not what they seem to be; he dramatizes the gap men drive between what they seem to be and what they are; he creates, like other poets, the very thing he exposes.

EXAMPLES OF SATIRIC IRONY

To make clear just how satiric irony operates, let us look at several examples. We can begin with an instance of scenic irony which makes clear the perspective inherent in all rhetorical and dramatic forms of irony. [In George Orwell's autobiographical novel *Down and Out in Paris and London,*] the speaker is describing his life as a dishwasher in a very expensive and very fashionable French hotel:

It was amusing to look round the filthy little scullery and think that only a double door was between us and the dining-room. There sat the customers in all their splendour—spotless table-cloths, bowls of flowers, mirrors and gilt cornices and painted cherubim; and here, just a few feet away, we in our disgusting filth. For it really was disgusting filth. There was no time to sweep the floor till evening, and we slithered about in a compound of soapy water, lettuce-leaves, torn paper and trampled food. A dozen waiters with their coats off, showing their sweaty armpits, sat at the table mixing salads and sticking their thumbs into the cream pots. The room had a dirty, mixed smell of food and sweat. Everywhere in the cupboards, behind the piles of crockery, were squalid stores of food that the waiters had stolen. There were only two sinks, and no washing basin, and it was nothing unusual for a waiter to wash his face in the water in which clean crockery was rinsing. But the customers saw nothing of this. There were a coco-nut mat and a mirror outside the dining-room door, and the waiters used to preen themselves up and go in looking the picture of cleanliness.

It is an instructive sight to see a waiter going into a hotel dining-room. As he passes the door a sudden change comes over him. The set of his shoulders alters; all the dirt and hurry and irritation have dropped off in an instant. He glides over the carpet, with a solemn priest-like air. I remember our assistant *maître d'hôtel,* a fiery Italian, pausing at the dining-room door to address an apprentice who had broken a bottle of wine. Shaking his fist above his head he yelled (luckily the door was more or less soundproof): "*Tu me fais _____*. Do you call yourself a waiter, you young bastard? You a waiter! You're not fit to scrub floors in the brothel your mother came from. Maquereau!" . . .

Then he entered the dining-room and sailed across it dish in hand, graceful as a swan. Ten seconds later he was bowing reverently to a customer. And you could not help thinking, as you saw him bow and smile, with the benign smile of the trained waiter, that the customer was put to shame by having such an aristocrat to serve him.

HOW IRONY BECOMES SATIRE

In the following excerpt from his book, The Anatomy of Criticism: Four Essays, *the influential literary critic Northrop Frye explains how satiric irony differs from irony in general. According to Frye, satire is irony that posits clear moral norms and attitudes.*

The chief distinction between irony and satire is that satire is militant irony: its moral norms are relatively clear, and it assumes standards against which the grotesque and absurd are measured. Sheer invective or name-calling ("flyting") is satire in which there is relatively little irony: on the other hand, whenever a reader is not sure what the author's attitude is or what his own is supposed to be, we have irony with relatively little satire. [Joseph] Fielding's *Jonathan Wild* is satiric irony: certain flat moral judgements made by the narrator . . . are in accord with the decorum of the work, but would be out of key in, say, [Gustav Flaubert's] *Madame Bovary.* Irony is consistent both with complete realism of content and with the suppression of attitude on the part of the author. Satire demands at least a token fantasy, a content which the reader recognizes as grotesque, and at least an implicit moral standards the latter being essential in a militant attitude to experience. Some phenomena, such as the ravages of disease, may be called grotesque, but to make fun of them would not be very effective satire. The satirist has to select his absurdities, and the act of selection is a moral act. . . .

Satire is irony which is structurally close to the comic: the comic struggle of two societies, one normal and the other absurd, is reflected in its double focus of morality and fantasy. Irony with little satire is the non-heroic residue of tragedy, centering on a theme of puzzled defeat.

Northrop Frye, *The Anatomy of Criticism: Four Essays.* Princeton, NJ: Princeton University Press, 1957.

Here the irony catches not a single individual but a society in its full pretense. On one side of the door it is assumed that men are civilized, mannerly, and prosperous, and that life is rich and orderly; on the other side we see the greasy reality on which this pretense rests, dirt, brutality, thievery, hunger, exhaustion. The door is "luckily" soundproof, so that the wealthy customers have no idea of the other face of their world, and the slaveys in the kitchen are either too dull to see the ironic gap or are forced by need to help maintain the pretense. But the satirist, though in this case he remains physically at the dirty sink, thinks himself into a position precisely at the soundproof door so that he can see and hear on both sides at once. He need not tell us that the world we think we live in is a sham, a play, and he need not denounce—though Orwell always goes on to do so—the blindness and selfishness that create a dream world and take it for real. His scenic irony has made all these points by creating an extended image in which seems and is are at dangerous variance.

The point at the soundproof door is the position the satiric ironist always occupies, though he may not always create the two components of the ironic situation and offer them side by side for inspection. Another type of satirist achieves his ironic effects by first describing whatever he despises and then peeling away the layers of pretense—manners, cosmetics, speech, clothes, faces—which cover the reality. [Roman satirist] Lucilius, who was, Horace tells us [in *Sermones*], the first man to compose formal verse satire, "stripped away the skin wherein everyone struts, flaunting his good looks in his neighbors' eyes while inwardly foul." Juvenal is a master of this technique. He offers a panorama of Imperial Rome, showing everywhere the masks of gravity, virtue, and patriotism with which the Romans cover themselves, and then in language so brutal that it seems literally to batter down all pretense, he shows us the terrible truth. [In his Sixth Satire] his wealthy matron wears beautiful green gems around her neck, pearls hang from her ears, her face is covered with cosmetics, her body is drenched in perfume, and she bathes daily in asses' milk. But,

> Through the last layer of the mudpack, from the first wash
> to a poultice,
> What lies under all this—a human face, or an ulcer?

Such techniques as this are so direct and crude that most of us would perhaps deny them the name of irony. And perhaps we would also feel that the related device of contrasting-revealing scenes, a scene at a London party followed by a scene in the jungles of the Amazon, would not qualify as irony. But the same appearance-reality conflict which is at the heart of irony is at work in these methods, though they leave something to be desired. They separate two things, appearance and reality, which are in fact one, for the seeming and being which the ironist shows us are not distinct in time and place but simultaneous. [Jonathan] Swift, I believe, claims for his own the introduction and refinement of the perfect ironic technique in which appearance and reality are collapsed into a single statement or image:

> Arbuthnot is no more my Friend,
> Who dares to Irony pretend;
> Which I was born to introduce,
> Refin'd it first, and shew'd its Use.
>
> ("Verses on the Death of Dr. Swift")

We may question whether Swift really introduced this kind of irony, but that he refined it and used it for maximum satiric effect, there is no question. The gap between appearance and reality is almost completely closed in the scene in which a group of fashionable ladies playing cards receive the news of Dean Swift's death:

> My female Friends, whose tender Hearts
> Have better learn'd to act their Parts,
> Receive the News in *doleful Dumps,*
> "The Dean is dead, (*and what is Trumps?*)
> "Then Lord have Mercy on his Soul.
> "(Ladies I'll venture for the *Vole.*)
> "Six Deans they say must bear the Pall.
> "(I wish I knew what *King* to call.)
> "Madam, your Husband will attend
> "The Funeral of so good a Friend.
> "No Madam, 'tis a shocking Sight,
> "And he's engag'd To-morrow Night!
> "My Lady Club wou'd take it ill,
> "If he shou'd fail her at *Quadrill.*
> "He lov'd the Dean. (*I lead a Heart.*)
> "But dearest Friends, they say, must part.
> "His Time was come, he ran his Race;
> "We hope he's in a better Place.

The ladies express pious sentiments and then return very quickly to what really interests them, the card game, so that they seem to assume a mask and then take it down. But as the scene progresses, the masks themselves come to reveal the reality. The speed of the four-beat line, the regularity of the rhythm, the patness of the rhymes, the conventional quality of the phrasing, and the subtle equation of people and cards, life and game—"He lov'd the Dean. (*I lead a Heart.*)," "My Lady Club," the rhyming of soul and vole—all combine to create people who play at life as they play at cards, or act their parts. The pretense itself contains the exposure of the ghastly truth of human nature which lies at the basis of the poem:

> In all Distresses of our Friends
> We first consult our private Ends.

If any slight distance still exists between seems and is in the cardplaying scene, it is closed altogether in such a speech as this in *A Modest Proposal:* "It is true a Child, *just dropt from its Dam,* may be supported by her Milk, for a Solar Year with little other Nourishment; at most not above the Value of two Shillings; which the Mother may certainly get, or the Value in Scraps, by her lawful Occupation of *Begging.*" The judicious phrasing, the reasonableness, the careful calculation, the scientific objectivity of this speech create the character of the Modest Proposer, a learned gentleman interested in the welfare of his nation, whose unawareness that he is talking about *people* leads inevitably to the proposition, made in the most reasonable manner, that both the food-shortage and the overpopulation of Ireland can be solved at once by selling the young children of the poor for food. Pose and reality are combined perfectly here to create a smug, emotionless, completely self-centered and dangerous dunce, who can solemnly assure us, and believe, that he has "not the least personal interest in endeavouring to promote this necessary Work," for he has no children by which he can "propose to get a single Penny; the youngest being nine Years old, and . . . [his] wife past Childbearing." This is what Swift is attacking: not just the cruelty of the social planner and the savage economic practices of the English landlords in Ireland, but the cruelty, and savagery, and heartlessnes which can offer themselves as clear-thinking philanthropy, disinterested patriotism, and sound economic practice.

Irony is the perfect device for rendering such self-deceit and hypocrisy, and the consistent use of irony in satire suggests that the tendency of dullness to create masks for itself is one of satire's principal subjects. Irony might, in fact, be called the master trope of satire which sums up all the other major figures used to construct the satiric world. I have, for the sake of discussion, separated out the major actions of dullness and the various rhetorical and scenic devices which render them. But in actual practice, though one tendency or another may dominate because it suits perfectly the particular brand of dullness being attacked—as the diminishing tendency suits an overconfident materialism—all of these tendencies are present simultaneously. Whenever ideas are reduced to things and life to mechanics in the satiric world, there always follows a magnification of the unworthy and a multiplication of the number of things. The result of this is inevitably the jumble. Taken together, these tendencies indicate a loss of some sensible belief about the nature of reality, and they lead on to a world in which the real is buried under messes of the unreal. But dullness always persists in believing that its conglomerations and pretensions are very real indeed, and it is just such a situation which irony catches and holds up for inspection.

Invective in Satire

David Worcester

Many people believe that anger is an important characteristic of satire. In the following selection, David Worcester argues that while anger and invective are common to satire, satirists use indirect methods to express that ire. According to Worcester, satirists rely on epithets, metaphors, similes, and other indirect forms rather than direct attacks, because the more blatant displays of anger tend to receive uncomfortable reactions instead of sympathy for the writer's views. By using less direct techniques, satirists are still able to make the object of their attack clear, but their readers do not feel that the writer's view has been forced upon them. Worcester was the author of *The Art of Satire*, from which the following essay has been selected.

Many persons instinctively shrink from satire as they might from a scorpion. Is not satire the expression of controversial heat, of venomous rancor, of the raw, negative emotion out of which humanity struggles to rise, age by age? Granted one dispensation, I hope to show that no such generalization is valid. A writer on lyric poetry feels no obligation to take account of newspaper jingles, yet a writer on satire finds it difficult to assume the same standard of excellence. Oceans of ink have been poured out in acrimonious and shocking libels and invectives; but so have oceans been spent on nauseous obituary verse and summer-verandah romances. In thinking of satire, we should consider the hundreds of works that have risen to the top. The millions below, graduated from acidulous gruel to a thick sludge of hell-broth, are interesting only insofar as they help to explain the principles of great satire.

How easily satirists acquire a bad name! Lucian, the Antichrist, deservedly torn to pieces by dogs; [François] Ra-

Excerpted from *The Art of Satire* by David Worcester, pp. 15–19, 24, 27 (Cambridge, MA: Harvard University Press, 1940). Copyright © 1940 by the President and Fellows of Harvard College. Reprinted with permission.

belais, the filthy mocker; [Jonathan] Swift, the inhuman misanthrope, not content with crucifying the women who loved him but bent on destroying the virtue and happiness of all mankind; one smiles on encountering these fancies, until damnable iteration brings on ironic melancholy. How little humanity, how little study, are needed to show that these and many other ill-treated satirists are the cleanest and brightest and merriest minded of men! Mark Twain remarked that the presence of only the Best People was enough to damn even heaven.

THE RANGE OF SATIRE

The content of satire is criticism, and criticism may be uttered as direct rebuke or as impersonal logic. Innumerable intermediate stages, by combining emotion and intellect in different proportions, lead from one pole of blind, human feeling to the opposite pole of divine, or inhuman, detachment. The spectrum-analysis of satire runs from the red of invective at one end to the violet of the most delicate irony at the other. Beyond either end of the scale, literature runs off into forms that are not perceptible as satire. The ultra-violet is pure criticism; the infra-red is direct reproof or abuse, untransformed by art.

In view of the pain, already mentioned, with which persons of delicate sensibilities are apt to regard satire, a large proportion of satiric literature might be expected to consist of direct attack, that is, open name-calling and nose-thumbing. Unquestionably many people hold this belief. To test it, Hugh Kingsmill's twin anthologies, *Invective and Abuse* and *More Invective,* may be consulted. Shuddering anticipation dies as the pages are turned and such old friends appear as . . . Prince Hal's mock-denunciation of Falstaff; [John] Donne's lyric "The Apparition"; . . . the King of Brobdingnag's Olympian summing-up of the English nation [in Jonathan Swift's *Gulliver's Travels*]; [Oliver] Goldsmith's almost jocular mock-epitaph, "Retaliation"; [Edmund] Burke's legal forensic against Warren Hastings; [John] Keats's anguished appeal to Fanny Brawne; and [Charles] Dickens' humorous description of Mr. Pickwick, routed from Bob Sawyer's rooms by Mrs. Raddle.

The editor writes:

Invective has been understood in this Anthology to mean direct verbal attack. Irony and satire are therefore, as far as

possible, excluded, though the line of demarcation is sometimes indistinct.

Here are grounds for wonder. Are the great verse-portraits to
be excluded from "satire" and Swift's master-strokes from
"irony"? Surely, invective must be stretched far beyond its
usual acceptation to include such mild and circuitous attacks. An occasional stinger does appear, like [Algernon]
Swinburne's letter to [Ralph Waldo] Emerson or [Robert]
Browning's lines to Edward FitzGerald. On the whole, however, wrath and hatred find little expression. The crux of the
matter lies in the words *"direct* verbal attack." It is the direct
attack that people expect to find in satire, particularly in
invective-satire, yet in almost every instance the emotion is
controlled, the blow is softened, and the approach is indirect.
Parody is not direct, nor are irony and mock-heroic. Their
whole force may be traced to the fact that they are indirect.

THE RELATIONSHIP BETWEEN ANGER AND SATIRE

The reason for the scarcity of direct invective in literature is
not far to seek. Anger is the most repellent of emotions. It is
acute discomfort to be present where a man has fallen into
a furious passion. If you are in such a situation, and the object of your acquaintance's rage has no connection with you,
you will experience an instinctive craving to escape into humor, to turn the painful situation into a ludicrous one. This
is done by withdrawing all sympathy from the blusterer and
by taking a more relativistic view of him as a lobster-faced
baboon in a fit. A little boy receiving a wigging will concentrate on a purple wart, if such there be, on his tormenter's
nose. Anger does not beget anger. Remember the artful self-
control of Mark Antony as he whipped the Roman populace
to a frenzy of rage by means of the cumulative irony of his
"So are they all, all honorable men."

Satire is the engine of anger, rather than the direct expression of anger. Before our sympathy is won, we must be freed
from the distress of witnessing naked rage and bluster. Like
Mark Antony, the artist must simulate coolness and detachment. Like the vaudeville marksman with his mirror, he
must look in one direction while he shoots in the opposite direction. To avoid the possibility of misunderstanding, it may
be emphasized that the actual text of an invective piece is the
only subject under discussion. A satire may be inspired by
rage; it may produce rage in its readers; but ninety-nine

times out of a hundred, rhetorical analysis of its language will reveal the widest differences between its style of attack and the style of a rattling good set-to between man and wife, or between a Communist lecturer and a member of the American Legion. To write in cold anger is to show detachment in language; to write in lofty anger is to affect disregard of an opponent; to write in cutting anger is to hold a victim in the icy grasp of irony. Mark Twain's *To the Person Sitting in Darkness* (1901) provoked a wilder furor than any other American satire before or since. His exposure of the looting and extortion practised by our missionaries in China was described by friends and foes as savage, blistering, and vitriolic. So it was—in its intent and in its effect, but not in its manner or its language.

Mark Twain prefaces his article with a newspaper dispatch, telling how a missionary had first collected 300 taels for each of 300 murdered native Christians and then had imposed a fine of thirteen times the total amount. The Catholics, having lost 680 in the uprising, demanded 750,000 strings of cash and 680 *Chinese heads!* Mark Twain's opening words are:

> By happy luck, we get all these glad tidings on Christmas Eve—just in time to enable us to celebrate the day with proper gayety and enthusiasm. Our spirits soar, and we find we can even make jokes: Taels, I win, Heads you lose.

With the same amused detachment, he proceeds in a leisurely way to roast the missionaries; but they are roasted by chilling irony, just as Bird's-Eye peas come to the pot already half cooked by the action of extreme cold. Nor does he depart at any time from the tone of irony. Clearly, some attention is due to the devices whereby detachment becomes the propelling force of strong emotion.

TWO TYPES OF INVECTIVE

Invective falls into two divisions. One lies within the province of satire, one outside it. A man who writes, "The asinine folly and loathsome immorality of the Government make decent citizens see red," is producing invective, but not satire. This gross invective, or abuse, is distinguished from satiric invective by direct, intense sincerity of expression. Satiric invective shows detachment, indirection, and complexity in the author's attitude.

There are exceptions to this judgment, but they are few.

When an invective-piece is sublime in utterance, when it reflects the thwarted passion of a great soul for the good, when it is sincere, and when its wrath is not too long-sustained, it is satire. In such an unusual conjunction, no psychological tricks are necessary to make the reader feel that the author has risen above his subject. Ezekiel denouncing sixth-century Jerusalem, Dante committing his contemporaries to hell, Juvenal pouring vitriol into his "Legend of Bad Women," as J.W. Mackail calls the sixth satire, these achieve satirical greatness with a minimum use of wit, irony, or burlesque. If we think a trifle less respectfully of Juvenal today than our grandfathers did, it is partly owing to our growing doubts of his sincerity. Dryden, who prefers him to Horace, bears out our point about the necessary brevity of invective:

> [Juvenal] drives his reader along with him; and when he is at the end of his way, I willingly stop with him. If he went another stage, it would be too far; it would make a journey of a progress, and turn delight into fatigue.

In general, philippic, jeremiad, and political diatribe lie outside the field of satire, because of their blunt directness. Likewise with the anathema, soberly committing its victim to hellfire. . . .

EPITHETS, SIMILES, AND EPIGRAMS

The next most direct mode of invective [is] the string of damaging epithets. "My opponent is a coarse, stupid, ugly man" is dull abuse, not satire. Heighten the language with bombast, novelty, or polysyllabic verbosity, and the satiric effect is instantly produced. . . .

It is but an inconsiderable step from calling a man fool or blackguard to calling him monkey or fox. There is less virulence, however, in the figurative than in the direct assault. This is not to say that a man would prefer the title of skunk to that of fool, for the degrees of intended censure are clearly different; but, other things being equal, men find simile and metaphor less offensive than plain epithet. A lady forced to choose between the alternatives would rather be described as a "weather-beaten she-dragon" than as a trouble-making old harridan, hag, virago, or trot. The metaphor opens the gates to imagination and suggestion. Moreover, it takes longer to manufacture and longer to digest, allowing anger to cool and wit to come into play. Whereas a man can harden himself before a torrent of abuse and shrug it off, his dignity can hardly survive a good Butlerian [referring to Samuel Butler] simile. . . .

To the curse, the epithet, the metaphor and the simile, used as rhetorical instruments of invective, the epigram may be added. Its requirements of compression and wit appear in [John] Rochester's well-known lines on Charles II:

> Here lies our Sovereign Lord the King;
>> Whose word no man relies on,
> Who never said a foolish thing,
>> Nor ever did a wise one.

A glance at these instruments in the order given reveals a progressive rise in intellectual content and in the author's detachment; correspondingly, there is a progressive decline in capacity to convey pure anger or hatred. At the same time, each instrument is capable of variation; without rhetorical heightening, the curse and the damaging epithet remain gross invective; with it, they pass over into invective satire. The epigram, based as it is upon wit, cannot drop back into gross invective without ceasing to be an epigram.

From each instrument to the next, there is an increase in detachment and complexity. Likewise there is a progressive increase in what may be called the "time-lag," that is, the interval between the perception of printed or spoken words and the full comprehension of their message. . . .

The writer of effective satiric invective keeps the abuse that he is attacking always before the reader's eyes. The light is clear, the object plain. Enough heightening and detachment are present to make the reader feel that he retains some independence, that he is not being forcibly fed, but not enough to obscure the object of satire.

Religion as a Target of Satire

Edward A. Bloom and Lillian D. Bloom

Edward A. Bloom and Lillian D. Bloom examine the
characteristics of religious satire in the following essay. According to the Blooms, much of this satire is
based on the satirist's effort to examine hypocrisy
and paradoxes while making people question religious creeds and ritual. For example, writers such as
Jonathan Swift and William Blake scorned the limitations and narrowness of religious views and consequently satirized those who blindly adhered to such
beliefs. The authors conclude that, while its tone and
purpose may be widely varied, religious satire ultimately aims to reveal people as they truly are,
stripped of all pretenses both religious and secular.
Edward A. Bloom was a professor of English at
Brown University, and Lillian D. Bloom was a professor of English at Rhode Island College. They were
the coeditors of *Addison and Steele, the Critical Heritage* and cowrote *The Variety of Fiction: A Critical
Anthology* and *Satire's Persuasive Voice.*

All religious satire, when well placed, causes discomfort, for
it attacks mores consecrated by time, culture, and awe. A
lancet for complacency, it cuts into mysteries that adhere to
religious systems and probes for answers to the presumably
inviolable. Illustrative of this truism, Blake parodied his former mentor [Swedish scientist and theologian Emanuel]
Swedenborg as an "Angel sitting at the tomb." His writings
Blake disparaged in the imagery of "linen clothes folded up"
uselessly, shrouds without meaning after death. The mystic
philosopher "shews the folly of churches, & exposes hypocrites," but despite the concession, Blake could no longer
accept as anything but error the limitations of one who "con-

Excerpted from *Satire's Persuasive Voice* by Edward A. Bloom and Lillian D. Bloom
(Ithaca, NY: Cornell University Press, 1979). Copyright © 1979 by Cornell University.
Used by permission of the publisher, Cornell University Press.

versed with Angels" yet "not with Devils who all hate religion." At other times more rompish and colloquial in his
iconoclasm, Blake ridiculed the excesses of organized worship. [In the poem "An Island in the Moon"] the voices of
"Mrs. Sinagain" and "Mrs. Sigtagatist" sound the praises of
such as "Mr. Huffcap" who "cry & stamp & kick & sweat, and
all for the good of their souls." Whether the souls are those
of the clergy or the congregation Blake—in a display of
satiric ambiguity that would have been congenial to [Robert]
Burns and [Edward] Gibbon—left the answer dangling. The
hypocrite and the pulpit-thumping parson remain as insep-
arable as Swift's strident Enthusiasts.

THE BASIS OF RELIGIOUS SATIRE

Religious satire has always thrived because spiritual and ec-
clesiastical uniformity contradicts diverse human nature
and man's tendency to reject or discredit whatever challenges his scheme of values and heritage. The vigor of opposition and inquiry alters in proportion to the intensity
with which the satirist feels committed to his belief or, for
that matter, disbelief. His vehicle, hence, is a rhetoric of protest that can range from laughter to rage, from comedy to
tragedy. Within this spectrum, further, his intention may
vary from the simple and clamorous to the multiple and deliberately obscure. Satire as harsh-sounding as that of
[Joseph] Hall and [John] Marston represents one function of
the mode; it amplifies personal biases often with a sem-
blance of bad temper. Occasional bursts of wit and metaphor
do little to modify abusiveness when the dominant tone is so
vengeful that the audience may transfer its sympathy from
satirist to ostensible culprit. And yet at the same level of personal involvement, the satirist may engage his enemy vin-
dictively but with a risible cleverness that entertains even
while it contends. [Andrew] Marvell, for instance, may not
convert us to his Puritan argument that sectarian multiplic-
ity premises the triumph of individual conscience and liberty; nevertheless we enjoy the suppleness with which he
dances about the heavy-breathing Parker.

Religious satire develops out of paradoxes, beginning with
the militant formulations designed to forward the teachings
of the Prince of Peace. The theme of brotherhood is celebrated, but frequently in a setting of derision or hostility and
denigration. The terms of such satire encourage intolerance;

if an equality of sects or of moral systems were admissible, most religious controversies would be harmlessly defused. The norm, rather, comes closer to that mockingly postulated by [Alexander] Pope [in his *An Essay on Criticism*]:

> (Thus wit, like faith, by each man is apply'd
> To one small sect, and all are damn'd beside.)

Humility, moreover, is fundamental to the Christian ethos; yet its satirical practitioners, whether Anglican, Catholic, or Deist, can be snide, even arrogant.

Authorial presumption—hard-voiced in a tonal idiom of deliberate crudity—marks Swift's refutation of enthusiasm, the fragmentary *Mechanical Operation of the Spirit.* Barely concealed in the persona of a carping letter-writer, Swift hounds the nonconformists, as Ehrenpreis comments, not "for having bodies, passions, faeces," but rather "for confusing these with religion, for describing themselves as inspired when they are windy, or as charitable when they are lustful." Enthusiastic preachers, the narrator says, argue in vain as to whether their gifts came from "possession, or inspiration." It is, he goes on, "a sketch of human vanity for every individual to imagine the whole universe is interested in his meanest concern. If he hath got cleanly over a kennel, some angel, unseen, descended on purpose to help him by the hand . . . this mystery of venting spiritual gifts is nothing but a trade." Every word that the commentator utters, as far as Swift is concerned, may be taken for his own literal certainties. The hyperbole and extravagant figuration merely add salt to these truths and preserve them in their satiric form. The letterwriter, then, is permitted to leave no doubt of his conscious purpose, which is to snuff out irretrievably (albeit vulgarly) confidence in the effulgence of the inner light.

FROM ABJURATION TO ASSAULT

Much of the satire that centers in religious debate owes its power to a paradoxical union of skepticism and authority. One incentive for satiric expression, indeed, springs from a desire to promote scruples as a counteraction to unreasoning acceptance of creed or ritual. At times, as in [John] Donne's third satire, the questioning is intrinsic, leading to a renewal and enforcement of faith. In other instances satirists may phrase questions that prompt disbelief, that deny any and all religious systems. This is the crisis into which the study of history drove Gibbon. Anticipating Bluphocks, the menippean vagabond of [Robert Browning's] *Pippa Passes,* Gibbon had "abjured all religions." And eventually, through the oblique intercession of a masked character, [James] Joyce passed radically beyond abjuration to an active assault upon Catholic dogma. He opened *Ulysses* with a disturbing integration of comic shock. "Stately, plump Buck Mulligan" looks like a vain, well-fed medieval prelate and lives up to his appearance as he intones the Mass and mocks the ritual. His irreverent parody sounds initially and uncomfortably like the whim of a world-weary college student.

The comedy—if such it be—vanishes almost immediately, however, with the arrival of a bereaved Stephen Dedalus, the "fearful Jesuit," as he is greeted. The shock mounts, for Mulligan confirms himself as a smugly satanic hypocrite who faults his friend for failure in the very Christian observance which he has been deriding: "You could have knelt down, damn it Kinch, when your dying mother asked you. . . . I'm hyperborean as much as you. But to think of your mother begging you with her last breath to kneel down and pray for her. And you refused. There is something sinister in you." The pun "hyperborean" clinches Mulligan's hypocrisy at several degrees of tension and meaning. It possesses first of all a bookish flavor that emphasizes the elegant sophisticate who struggles to maintain the pose. As an uncommon word, further, it makes us grope through its ambiguities, for "hyperborean" has associations shifting from the specific to the mythic.

At one level, then, the word literalizes the fact that the two young men dwell in a northern region. It is simply an academic way of saying that they are countrymen with the same national or social traditions. More subtly, however, Mulligan wants Dedalus to assert their moral affinity. Since the fabulous Hyperboreans were a happy race situated beyond the north in a land of sunshine, Mulligan implies that he and Dedalus stand apart from ordinary men and that, by extension, both are imbued with the good of their virtuous environment. The irony is that Mulligan, the self-identified hypocrite, attributes to himself qualities that belong to Dedalus. The makeup of the hypocrite contains no virtue, whereas Dedalus, who respects the age-old force of the religion he has forsworn, eschews deceit. Mulligan, standing apart only through his capacity for affectation, is happy, as Dedalus—the eternal seeker—is not. From the very outset, therefore, Joyce grants his fiction freedom, permits it to plummet and rise, to move from parody to sham, from tragedy to blasphemy, all and always in a need to express, however indirectly, his quest for an inner truth beyond the ambience of religious discipline.

The trail from [Roman satirist] Lucian to Joyce continues a long one but it is blazed plainly with its diversity of tone and theme and purpose. Religious satire, we have seen, is often unwelcome, beginning with the biblical warning that only "fools make a mock at sin." Obversely, however, such satire has its defenders who perhaps even more frequently urge it as a way of appealing to sinners and dissidents. Theologians such as Stillingfleet and Swift, for example, hammer away at those who have not come around to an Anglican piety. Members of the Dissenting laity, such as Marvell and [Daniel] Defoe, engage in comparable methods of persuasion to affirm their own attitudes of faith and conscience. "They are all proponents of an absolute outlook: each serves as a disputant either rigidly for or rigidly against certain principles of ceremony and belief. But others promote a judicious temperance. Like Donne, they acknowledge the inconsistencies of human conduct and temptation that may inhibit spiritual commitment. They rely upon a call to reason as well as moral passion. To doubt, they would say, can be efficacious, but it must be wise doubt.

And also in a religious context there remain those scoffers—Gibbon, Joyce, and the like—who do not make a mock at sin, yet who do reject institutionalized piety. Reminiscent of writers like Erasmus and Burns but delighting in their iconoclasm, they stress the incidence of hypocrisy and religious egocentricity without turning their backs on the concept of brotherhood. Nevertheless, by means of ironic language and imagery each of these satirists intends to arouse moral antipathies; each exhibits a longing to repudiate corruption and to exalt the good, whatever its definition, as a way of life. As synthesized by [Samuel Taylor] Coleridge: "When serious satire commences, or satire that is felt as serious, however comically drest, the free laughter ceases; it becomes sardonic." Following the Coleridgean premise, we may correlate serious with religious satire, which aims to see man for what he really is. To be seen thus, man must be stripped of all outer disguises, like Lemuel Gulliver standing naked before the master of the Houyhnhnms. Or, it may not be too much to say, like man standing before his God.

Satire and Politics

Leonard Feinberg

Politics are a common target in satire. In the following viewpoint, Leonard Feinberg explains how
satirists view politics from both a radical and conservative perspective. Regardless of their political beliefs, writes Feinberg, satirists tend to attack those
who disagree with them, rather than defend their
own views. However, these attacks do not necessarily imply that the satirist supports the opposing view.
Oftentimes, satirists are merely reacting against
those views which are inconsistent with their own.
Feinberg also argues that like most people, satirists
are inconsistent in their political positions, with
many changing their philosophy as they age. Feinberg is a professor emeritus of English at Iowa State.
His books include *Introduction to Satire, Sinclair
Lewis as a Satirist,* and *The Satirist: His Temperament, Motivation, and Influence,* the book from
which the following article has been selected.

Because they often criticize the *status quo*, satirists have been
called "radicals" by some scholars. Other scholars insist that
satirists are conservatives, who attack deviations from the
norm (or the theoretical norm) of their society. Each theory
is convincing, and would be even more convincing were it
not for the fact that there have actually been radical, liberal,
conservative, and reactionary satirists. Furthermore, there
have been conservative satirists in liberal periods and in conservative periods; and there have been liberal satirists in liberal periods and in conservative periods.

The satirist is likely to be skeptical about most social institutions. Even satirists who are staunch partisans of specific political systems do not pretend that those systems are
perfect. And from time to time satirists change their political
affiliations, implying that they are not as profoundly con-

vinced as some of their works indicate they are. Samuel
Johnson was a Tory, Charles Churchill was a Whig;
[Jonathan] Swift, like them an eighteenth-century satirist,
had been a Whig and became a Tory. Ben Franklin has been
praised by conservatives and liberals. Some satirists definitely chose one political party or another; others vacillated
among parties in and out of power; still others never committed themselves.

UNDERSTANDING THE SATIRIST'S REASONING

In discussing the politics of satirists it is well to remember
that by his very nature the satirist is an attacker rather than
a defender. Criticism functions by exposing the wrong,
rather than by praising the right. For the satirist it is less a
problem of morality than of temperament and technique.
Satire specializes in incongruities and weaknesses and inadequacies. For that reason even when he takes the conservative position (as he often does), the satirist concentrates
not on defending the *status quo* but on attacking critics of
that *status quo*. When he takes the "radical" position, he criticizes the weaknesses of his society. Because every society
offers innumerable opportunities for criticism, the satirist is
more likely to seem liberal or radical than conservative or
reactionary. In practice, however, few satirists have been
sufficiently courageous, or sufficiently radical, to attack the
basic economic or political organization of their society.

Since the satirist is often motivated by his feelings rather
than by his reason it is not safe to assume that simply because he criticizes something he approves of the obvious alternative. It is quite wrong to suppose that because George
Orwell ridiculed the excesses of totalitarianism, in *Animal
Farm* and *1984,* he approved of capitalism; he was, in fact,
an active Socialist. It is a mistake to think, as many critics
did, that because Sinclair Lewis was a vociferous critic of
middle class Americans he advocated some other way of life.
Lewis himself repeatedly admitted that he liked middle class
Americans and their way of life best of all. Nor should Aldous Huxley's criticism of the philosophic, scientific, and
economic trends of the twentieth century be interpreted as
approval of the logical alternatives. Huxley's mystic answers
are quite different from the conventional ones.

The impetus that Voltaire gave to the revolution in France
is widely recognized. But Voltaire himself accepted the the-

ory of monarchy and, in Schilling's words, "was distrustful of popular movements, of sudden and violent changes in a social scheme of things that had treated him generously most of his life." G.K. Chesterton, who in 1899 had called England an imperialistic bully, in World War I supported England as a "heroic defender of Christian civilization against Prussianism." On the other hand, as Irvine points out, Bernard Shaw supported England in 1899 "as taking a necessary step toward world peace," and in 1914 criticized her "as sharing in the guilt and stupidity of an unnecessary war."

CHANGING OR VAGUE POLITICAL VIEWS

Satirists, like other men, have on occasion changed their political views, usually proceeding from an early liberalism to an elderly or middle-aged conservatism. The customary shift is from adolescent criticism of society to middle-aged defense of society. Among satirists who followed this pattern, Sydney Smith was for many years an aggressive liberal protestant against reactionary Tory procedures; but as he aged, Smith turned more and more toward a conservative position. W.H. Auden sympathized with Communism in the thirties, liberalism in the forties, and conservatism in the fifties. And John Dryden went through a number of changes which coincided with changes in the political climate of England after the Restoration.

Charles Dickens' politics have led critics to contradictory conclusions. Marxist T.A. Jackson insists that Dickens was practically a Communist; conservative G.K. Chesterton insists that Dickens was a conservative. George Orwell and Edmund Wilson find elements of both radicalism and conservatism in Dickens. Monroe Engel concludes that Dickens is a "radical" in the sense of going to the root of things, but definitely not a Marxist, being "anti-deterministic" and "opposed to any extremism." Dickens attacked Chartism, the radical political movement of his own time. Yet he sympathized with many of the Chartist objectives and exposed in his books the social evils of Victorian England.

Some satirists have avoided taking definite political positions. Edgar Johnson, contrasting Ovid to [Lord George Gordon] Byron, notes that Ovid's work "had none of those political overtones . . . no paeans to liberty, no blasts of indignation against oppression and tyranny." Analyzing [Henrik] Ibsen's opinions, Thompson writes, "It is characteristic of his ironic temper that in reading Cicero Ibsen sympathized with the object of the orator's invective, the rebel against order and respectability." Ibsen may have been sympathetic, but he never expressed any rebellion against the political systems of his own time. Max Eastman says of Artemus Ward that "many of his opinions were a mere, unimaginative standing-pat on the *status quo* . . . his attitude toward the Mormons was Philistine. Upon the subject of woman's rights he was an ordinary male bigot. . . . Politically he was vague." Eastman feels that Ward was telling the truth when he said, "I have only drifted with the current, which has carried me gaily on of its own accord." And Thackeray showed as a student at Cambridge "the same mistrust of extremes in political and religious questions that he showed in later life." When he stood for Parliament, it was as an Independent.

In an article on satirists in politics, Dr. [W.A.] Pannenborg notes that of the eleven satirists he classified as "extroverts," five were involved in political activity—[Pierre] Beaumarchais, [Daniel] Defoe, [August] Kotzebue, [Nicole] Machiavelli, and Voltaire. Pannenborg suggests that politically active individuals are far more likely to make use of irony than the average man, that the typical politician tends to be ambitious, imperious, and unreliable, and that these five satirists were ambitious, imperious, and unreliable.

SATIRE AND THE STATUS QUO

If [Henri] Bergson's view (laughter is society's way of punishing nonconformists and keeping them in line) is correct, satire is basically conservative and satirists are conservatives. In support of this theory, [Wolfgang] Zucker points out that the hero who challenges the existing order and becomes the standard bearer of a revolt is likely to be the "protagonist of a tragedy." The criticism of the *status quo* by humorists and satirists is a safe one, says Zucker, "where the comedian ridicules some old institutions . . . the old hierarchy has already cracked up and the audience applauds its own victory." But it would be extremely difficult to prove that all of the objects of satiric criticism have actually "cracked up."

A related theory states that laughter at the expense of the *status quo* permits a healthy letting-off of steam; the laughers understand that they are indulging in a letting-off of steam, and that the criticized institutions will not be changed. In the Fool's Day celebrations popular during the Middle Ages, the Fools and their patrons took prominent part; "however," notes Enid Welford, "in France, as was natural, the royal fools were noted champions of orthodoxy." The newspapers and periodicals with the largest circulation in the United States and England are today the aggressively conservative ones, whose caustic ridicule of innovators and idealists seems to please their reading public.

"The satirist claims," says Robert Elliott, "with much justification, to be a true conservative. Usually . . . he operates within the established framework of society, accepting its norms . . . as the standard against which to judge the follies he sees. He is the preserver of tradition." Bernard Shaw once said, "In really contemporary situations, your genius is ever one part genius and ninety-nine parts Tory." [Jonathan] Swift, [Alexander] Pope, [Samuel] Johnson, [John] Gay, [John] Arbuthnot, [John] Dryden, [William] Gilbert, and [George] Canning are prominent English conservatives. "Orthodoxy is my doxy," announced Sam Johnson. Russell Kirk gives Chesterton and Belloc credit for nourishing the conservative impulse, although he limits his approval: "But [Hillaire] Belloc and [G.K.] Chesterton were only auxiliaries of conservatism." Kirk braises James Russell Lowell's conservatism, disregarding his early radicalism and explaining that Lowell's deviations from tradition were due to special conditions in the North of his time. Lowell wrote in a letter, "I was always a natural Tory, and in England should be a staunch one." Roy Campbell, an avid disciple of Wyndham Lewis, was a militant fascist.

Sei-Shonagon's *Pillow-Book* is a classic example of Japanese satire. Her humor, R.H. Blyth says, "is peculiarly Japanese in that it springs from the genius she has for the perception of the fitness of things." French remarks that "it is idle to reproach Chaucer for the conservatism which is so pronounced a feature of his temperament," and to complain that he is not clearly aware of the rottenness of medieval institutions. And W.F. Taylor observes that during the nineteenth century the "native American humorists . . . customarily assumed the prudential code of the middle class, and often explicitly satirized violations of that code."

The inconsistency of a conservative satirist's position is recognized by Cazamian: Jonathan Swift "stirred up a deep and secret unrest in the minds of those in power during his

time . . . despite the conformity of his declarations and principles." Yet the basic conservatism of Swift seems unques-
tionable. In his sermon on "mutual subjection," Swift
warned the poor against committing the sin of "murmuring
and repining, that God hath dealt his blessings unequally to
the sons of man." Swift regarded the inferior position of
most men a necessity in God's order. "For a person of Swift's
conservative habits of mind," Louis Landa says, this theory
seemed perfectly acceptable; Landa shows that although
Swift was a strong supporter of the Charity School movement, he insisted that these schools train their pupils only
for "the very meanest trades" and as domestic help. Swift
warned against the economic danger of preparing people
above their station in life.

As with Voltaire and Swift, there is evidence of inconsistency in the conservatism of Dr. Johnson. George B. Hill
quotes a number of "radical" statements by Johnson which
might have "scared the city Tories." Johnson's acceptance of
the theory of subordination and his insistence on the fundamental principles of Tory philosophy made him a fairly
safe man to be given a pension. Yet Johnson was unortho-
dox enough to write: "No scheme of policy has in any country yet brought the rich and poor on equal terms into the
court of judicature." At another time he said, "a decent pro-
vision for the poor is the true test of civilization." His religious and ultraconservative father, a man similar to the father against whom Anatole France rebelled, became for
Samuel Johnson a symbol of dignity and respect; Johnson
remained a confirmed Tory and a devout layman. One of
Johnson's early teachers, John Hunter, was a confirmed Ja-
cobite,[1] and the climate of opinion in Lichfield was strongly
conservative. At Oxford, where Johnson went in 1728, the
same tradition prevailed.

CONSERVATIVE VERSUS REACTIONARY

On the political continuum, a line between conservatives and
reactionaries cannot be sharply drawn. If, however, we are to
regard those who are most insistent on a return to the past as
representative of the reactionary point of view, Juvenal is a
reactionary. He complains about the privileges extended to

---

1. Jacobites were supporters of Roman Catholic King James II and his descendants in
their claim to the British throne.

former slaves, the impudence of actors and merchants and gladiators, the prevalence of Greeks and other foreigners in Rome, and the loss of respect for old families. Juvenal says nothing about the advantages of political freedom in the old republic, before the tyrannical emperors of his own day took power; he rants about moral decay, but carefully avoids direct criticism of cruel and degenerate kings.

If H.L. Mencken were judged solely by his writings, he too would have to be regarded as a reactionary. His espousal of the "superman" theory of Nietzsche, his acceptance in human society of the law of the jungle, his contempt for democracy, all put Mencken in the category of political reactionaries. He ridiculed Christianity, he hated socialism, and he despised "humanitarianism."

Aristophanes, colorful and vituperative, was also a reactionary. He was always fighting for the good old days, when families like his own were given proper recognition. A rich man and a landowner, he had personal as well as philosophic reasons for objecting to the political and economic policies of the democratic parties in power. He was courageous in expressing that objection, but it was the objection of a conservative critic.

Whether T.S. Eliot belongs in the conservative or reactionary grouping is debatable. Russell Kirk puts him in "the tradition of Burke." Eliot's desire for a graded society, his opposition to democracy, and his partisanship for the elite certainly put him far to the right of center.

Evelyn Waugh claims that "there is no political party in existence . . . sufficiently (in the strictly literal sense of the word) reactionary" for him to join. He maintains that he is at least two hundred years behind the times and in his comments on modern politics approves only of fascist governments. Waugh urges a return to the medieval way of life, with greater respect for the aristocracy and the Catholic Church. In a one-man war against modern civilization, he writes with a pen which has to be dipped in ink, refuses to learn how to drive a car, and sends letters to neighbors instead of using the telephone. Waugh is rebelling against a liberal society, liberal religion, and liberal politics.

In an essay called "The Socialist," Ambrose Bierce described the typical socialist as a stupid, often immoral, intellectually sick incompetent who wants to level society down to its lowest denominator. Bierce attacked all organized attempts of civilized society to care for its members. No system of political philosophy appealed to him, but inasmuch as he castigated liberal institutions far more vehemently than conservative ones it seems safe to call Bierce a reactionary.

Shortly before he died, Dean Inge remarked that he believed neither in "heaven, hell, nor the British socialists." And Mikes calls Stephen Leacock "a republican who genuinely approved of the monarchy."

INCONSISTENCY IN LIBERAL SATIRE

Just as there is reason to doubt the consistency of conservative satirists, there are grounds for questioning the consistency of liberal satirists. They too have often contradicted themselves. Even the liberalism of Anatole France, who late in his career was lauded by communists, has been questioned. Marcel LeGoff says, "His socialism is not an urge of the heart, nor an organizing thought, it is but the manifestation of his irony." Chevalier dismisses the liberal activities of France (. . . socialism, pacifism) as peripheral. France, however, reverses the usual order of development, and proceeds from the conservatism of his early years to the liberalism of his later period. He said, before World War I, "I do not wish for socialism, but I do not fear it." During the war he expressed sympathy for Russian communism, but towards the end of his life he was, according to Shanks, completely disillusioned and disgusted with all revolutions.

Sydney Smith was an active and courageous Whig most of his life, especially when it was politically unwise to be one. But after 1830, when the Whigs came into power, he became more and more conservative, saying, "I find an utter inability of fighting for either party." By the time he died, Smith had expressed doubts about the wisdom of extending the franchise. Yet he had spent most of his life fighting for liberal causes, at the expense of his own promotion in the church.

Sinclair Lewis had never been very radical, and by the end of his life veered towards conservatism. As early as his Nobel Prize Address in 1929, he described himself, correctly, as "a writer whose most anarchistic assertion has been that America, with all her wealth and power, has not yet produced a civilization good enough to satisfy the deepest wants of human creatures." P.G. Wodehouse admits, "I never was interested in politics. I'm quite unable to work up any kind of belligerent feeling." And there is good reason to believe that Charlie Chaplin's criticism of society is based less on Marxist political theory than on an individualistic, anarchistic revolt against all kinds of authority.

Among liberal satirists, covering a wide range of "liberalism," are Shaw, Hugh MacDiarmid, John Kendrick Bangs, H.G. Wells, George Orwell, and J.B. Priestley, who announced in 1951, "I am not a socialist." To these may be added Charles Churchill, John Wolcot, Lord Byron, Addison, and Steele, and, with some reservations, Hugo, Vondel, Franklin, Freneau, and Trumbull.

The radical of one generation becomes, it has been often observed, the conservative of the next. That wild radical of the early twentieth century, Shaw, is today dismissed as an old-fashioned Fabian[2] socialist.

---

2. The Fabian Society was a socialist society founded in London in 1883. Its members, which included George Bernard Shaw, wanted a democratic socialist state established in Great Britain.

The Treatment of Women in Satire

Matthew Hodgart

In the following essay, Matthew Hodgart details the
depiction of women throughout the history of satire.
Hodgart examines works that range from early
Greek plays to eighteenth-century social criticism—
and then illustrates how the various male authors
portray women. According to Hodgart, women have
been a frequent target of male satirists for two reasons. First, women are convenient scapegoats. Second, satire enables men to express the resentment
they feel when confronted by any display of female
power. However, not all of early satire directed at
women is negative in its tone. While Juvenal and
Jonathan Swift depicted women as lascivious and
grotesque, Aristophanes and Geoffrey Chaucer were
among the satirists who acknowledged female independence and strength. Hodgart was a professor of
English at the University of Sussex in England and
the author of several books, including biographies of
Samuel Johnson and James Joyce and *Satire,* the
source of the following selection.

Since men enjoy the advantages of physical strength, intellectual energy, political power and wealth, and until recently
also those of legal status and education, it seems unnecessary as well as unchivalrous for them to have written as
much satire on women as they have. A partial explanation
has been offered by Dr [Samuel] Johnson: 'As the faculty of
writing has been chiefly a masculine endowment, the reproach of making the world miserable has been always
thrown upon the women'. He reminds us of the simple fact
that nearly all satire, like the greater part of all literature,
has been written by men. He also implies that since the

Excerpted from *Satire* by Matthew Hodgart (New York: McGraw-Hill, 1969). Copyright
1969 by Matthew Hodgart.

world *is* miserable, the blame is always being thrown on some person or persons: if not on the political party currently in power, or the capitalists or the workers or the Jews, then on the scapegoat most conveniently to hand, which is the female sex. The fact that, unlike racial minorities or political régimes, women cannot be banished or abolished but are here for ever is therefore a deeper source of irritation to the male satirist as well as a more persistent stimulus to writing than those produced by any other subject. The correct analogy to be drawn, moreover, is with the Jews and the workers (or slaves), not with the rulers: women are among the ruled, or as the sociologists say, they form an under-privileged subculture in nearly all societies. The satirist who pursues this topic runs little risk, except at the hands of his own wife, who may like Chaucer's Wife of Bath, fling his odious book into the fire. Men perhaps feel some guilt about their exploitation of women's inferiority, but they also feel resentment, because with all their advantages their power over women is far from complete, and in some ways women may have power over them. This resentment lies behind much anti-feminist literature, as it does behind much that masters have written about servants. Here again Johnson is helpful, provided that we turn his aphorism upside down: 'nature has given women so much power that the law has wisely given them little' is a paradoxical way of saying 'although the law, and education, the economic system etc. have deprived women of so much power, they are still formidable opponents in the sex-war'. The traditional weapons of the sex, according to a saying quoted by the Wife of Bath, are deceit, weeping and spinning: 'Fallere, flere, nere, dedit Deus in muliere'. Deceit includes cuckoldry, a shaming blow to the male ego; weeping implies that feminine weakness and sensibility may have some inhibiting effect on masculine brutality; and for 'spinning' we should now read 'knitting', which is symbolic of the woman's withdrawal of her attention into household tasks or into exclusively female society—the man, his advances and complaints ignored, loses self-esteem. An even more potent weapon is the *Lysistrata* tactic or the refusal of sexual consent, by which the errant Greek husbands in the play were soon brought to heel—a fantasy, but near enough to the truth, since sexual pleasure without consent or co-operation is hardly pleasure at all. To resentment there must be added a certain fear which men have of women, even without admitting it: the ancient awe of prehistoric religions, most of which included the cult of the Great Mother; the worship of the White Goddess, who according to [English poet and scholar] Robert Graves is the woman in her triple role as mother, lover, and layer-out of the corpse; the terror aroused by the witch.

The reality behind what men have written about women is an ambivalence of feeling, which includes deep antagonism. This reality has been elaborated and disguised by a variety of myths; in fact, as Simone de Beauvoir reminds us in *Le Deuxième Sexe*, almost everything written about women is myth and myth made by man. Taken seriously, sex antagonism is the stuff of several great tragic plays and novels, by Euripides, [August] Strindberg, [Samuel] Richardson, Choderlos de Laclos and others; taken lightly, it is the basis of most comedies of manners e.g. by [William] Congreve or [George Bernard] Shaw; but taken moralistically it has inspired satire. The opposite of satire is the encomium, the formal work 'in praise of women', which became a formal genre in the Middle Ages, like Chaucer's *Legend of Good Women.* The encomium embodies myth: it sets out to praise the ideal woman, but in fact prescribes how women, in men's opinion, ought to behave. The story of patient Griselda, whose incredible sufferings at the hands of her tyrannous husband were duly rewarded, is an extreme example, but it was recounted solemnly as a model of docility. The encomium also reflects the double standard of sexual morality which has prevailed until recently in civilised society: women have been expected to be more chaste than men, as well as more modest in dress and demeanour. The fuss made by the moralists about women's fashions, cosmetics and coiffure is based only partly on the very reasonable grounds of expense; it also voices the suspicion that such adornments are meant to allure men other than the husband. Satire on women is a comic recording of deviations from the ideal set up by the encomium; and traditionally it has been centred on the cardinals of docility, chastity and modesty. . . .

GREEK AND ROMAN ATTITUDES TOWARD WOMEN

Aristophanes, although he treats the subject of sex with unashamed indecency, is at heart sympathetic to women. The *Lysistrata* is aimed at the militarist party, not at the women who try to stop the war so intelligently and generously. Elsewhere he praises women for being more conservative than men (which is true) and therefore not so likely to be drawn into the new-fangled and wrong-headed schemes of the Athenian democracy. In the *Ecclesiazusae,* or 'Women in Parliament' as Jack Lindsay translates it, which is yet another play built around a saturnalian reversal of the social order, he praises as much as he satirises, expressing charmingly through Praxagora the ambivalence which the best writers on this subject seem to show.

PRAXAGORA:
You won't find *them* (the women) I warrant, in a hurry
Trying new plans. And would it not have saved
The Athenian city had she let alone
Things that worked well, nor idly sought things new?
They roast their barley, sitting, as of old:
They on their heads bear burdens, as of old:
They keep their Thesmophoria, as of old:
They bake their honied cheesecakes, as of old:
They victimize their husbands, as of old:
They still secrete their lovers, as of old . . .

There is no ambivalence in Juvenal. His sixth satire is a scabrous diatribe against the vices and follies of contemporary Roman women. His class bias is noteworthy: all his examples are taken from the ladies of high society, whose wrongdoings are highly expensive ones. He has thus produced yet another tract against luxury and decadence, in contrast to the primitive simplicity of the Golden Age, and to the chastity and modesty of republican Rome. He describes with verve fashionable ladies who take a fancy to actors or run away with gladiators, the empress Messalina who took her turn in the brothel; then turning to folly, he ridicules women who beguile their time with athletics, music, gluttony, literature and fortune-telling. (I confess to finding his female athlete, flushed after her fencing exercises, rather attractive, but we are not supposed to think so.) He ends on a more sinister note, where his satire puts on the buskin of Tragedy, with abortion and the poisoning of husbands: there is a Clytemnestra[1] in every street. . . .

1. Clytemnestra was a character in Greek mythology. She was the wife of King Agamemnon of Mycenae, who led the Greek forces during the Trojan War. Clytemnestra's anger at her husband, after he sacrificed one of their children to enable his ships to sail to Troy, led her to take a lover, Aegisthus. When Agamemnon returned from Troy with his mistress, the Trojan princess Cassandra, Clytemnestra and Aegisthus killed them both. They ruled Mycenae for seven years until Clytemnestra's son Orestes killed them.

MEDIEVAL SATIRES ON WOMEN

In the fabliaux[2] the old themes of women's wiles are being transformed into literary satire. Meanwhile a huge literature concerning marriage and its problems was growing cumulatively, each author repeating and adding to the material of his predecessors, and this too became gradually transformed from moral homily into imaginative narrative. Around the kernel of Theophrastus, Juvenal and St Jerome there grew successively the *De Nugis Curialium* of the twelfth-century Walter Map, the *Lamentations* of the thirteenth-century Matheolus (a cleric who lost his benefice because of his marriage), the second part of the *Roman de la Rose* by Jean de Meung, the fourteenth-century *Miroir de Mariage* by Chaucer's friend Eustache Deschamps and finally Chaucer's triumphant use of this material in the *Canterbury Tales*. Jean de Meung, who has been called the Voltaire of the Middle Ages, wrote a long and diffuse sequel to Guillaume de Lorris's courtly allegory of the rose, which offers a kind of encyclopedia of learned subjects: his object was to take such learning away from the church's monopoly and offer it to the laity in clear vernacular French verse. His satire ranges widely, but anti-clericalism is his main theme: his brutal portrait of the hypocritical friar Faux-Semblant, who exposes his tricks in a cynical monologue, is the model for Chaucer's Friar and Pardoner. When he turns to the subject of women, his drift is two-fold: first, to repeat the traditional slanders, not as an awful warning, but as realistic comedy; and secondly to attack the church's doctrines of celibacy. There are long speeches by Nature and Genius, who attack virginity and ask every man to do his duty in propagating the species. De Meung makes a spirited defence of the flesh and of natural sexuality, in anticipation of the spirit of Boccaccio's *Decameron* and *The Wife of Bath's Prologue*. The model for Chaucer's Wife of Bath is De Meung's *La Vieille*, or the Duenna, the experienced woman who passes on her amorous secrets to the younger generation, telling the truth about her scandalous life without shame or repentance:

> By God! it pleases me still, when I think over my past life: it delights me much in my thought and my limbs feel their vigour return, when I remember the good time I had and the

2. Fabliaux are rhymed stories in verse that were popular entertainment in thirteenth-century France.

> gay life, which my heart now so longs for; my whole body
> grows young again, when I recall it to mind.

Or as the Wife of Bath puts it:

> But, Lord Christ! whan that it remembreth me
> Upon my yowthe, and on my jolitee,
> It tikleth me aboute myn herte mote,
> Unto this day it dooth myn herte boote
> That I have had my world as in my tyme.

Chaucer surpasses de Meung in richness of invention and
complexity of irony. The Wife of Bath rehearses the preachers' views on virginity, only to refute them: the body was
made for love and fertility or 'engendrure' she says, quoting
scripture gaily, for 'God bad us for to wexe and multiplye',
while Solomon and the Patriarchs had many wives. Virginity may be the ideal state, but there is a place for everything:
Christ did not tell every man to sell all he hath:

> He spak to them that wolde lyve parfitly
> And lordynges, by your leve, that am nat I.

She tells her life-story with zest, describing racily how she
dealt with her five husbands, 'How piteously a-nyght I made
them swynke (work)'. She repeats the traditional satires,
from the Book of Proverbs, St Jerome and the rest—her fifth
husband used to read them out aloud until she burnt his
book—only to brush them aside:

> Thou sayest that dropping houses, and eke smoke
> And chiding wyves maken men to flee
> Out of hir owen hous—a benedicitee!

She produces her horoscope; since she was born under
Venus but with the evil influence of Mars, she has been driven by the planets into a life of carnality: so

> Alas, alas, that ever love was sin!

The Wife of Bath is an independent bourgeoise, who by her
skill in weaving could make enough money to do as she
liked: hence her confident feminism when she comes to the
central issue of the satirical tradition, which is women's
domination or as Chaucer calls it 'maistrie' (mastery). Her
solution for marital happiness is for the husband to hand
over all authority to the wife; and this is the moral of the
witty and graceful tale which she then tells to the pilgrims.
This subject is explored at length in the group of Canterbury
Tales that follow, until what one feels is Chaucer's personal
view, a humanist one, is put forward with modest irony in

the Franklin's Tale: neither husband nor wife is to have the 'mastery' but marriage is to be a partnership of equals. Chaucer has turned satire against the satirists: he accepts the absurdities and grossnesses of sexuality and marriage with ironic good humour, as the richest part of life's comedy. Neither defending nor blaming the Wife of Bath he presents her as triumphant in her animal vitality. As James Joyce wrote of his own Molly Bloom, who is an even richer character, she is 'sane full amoral fertilisable untrustworthy engaging limited prudent indifferent Weib. "Ich bin das Fleisch das stets bejaht!"'[3]

On this topic, as on others the Middle Ages are repetitive. As the tradition goes on, only a few works of the fifteenth century show anything to equal Chaucer's genius. . . .

THE BEGINNING OF FEMALE EMANCIPATION

The last time in English that the note of medieval preacher's horror of the flesh was sounded was in the most disgusting poems of [Jonathan] Swift and in his description of the female Yahoo; but here we are moving from satire to the borders of the psychopathic grotesque. [Alexander] Pope is the best of the verse satirists [of the eighteenth century] to comment on women with the right blend of malice and sympathy. The moral of his *Rape of the Lock* (1714) is ostensibly 'Vanity, vanity, all is vanity, and this delicious mock-Homeric epic sees women as the exemplars of vanity. Just as the plot of the poem is the exaltation of a trivial event into a great action, so the basic rhetorical device is zeugma, the absurd linking together of the trifling and the serious: 'When husbands or when lapdogs breathe their last', 'To stain her honour or the new brocade', 'Puffs, powders, patches, bibles, billets-doux': to Pope's heroine and to women in general these things are equally important. The poem states simultaneously that women are responsible for the minor vanities of civilised life, and that it is precisely these trifles, whether silverware or porcelain, that give life its grace; it is a triumphant celebration of these minor arts as well as a courteous mockery of those who give them exaggerated value. Women are both absurd and vulnerable, the symbols both of vanity and of ideal beauty:

Oh if to dance all night and dress all day

3. "I am the flesh that always affirms."

Charm'd but old age and the smallpox away
Who would not scorn what housewife's care produce,
Or who would learn one earthly thing of use.

Some years later Pope returned to the subject in *Moral Essays,* Epistle II to Mrs M. Blount, also known as *On the Character of Women* ('Most women have no characters at all'). This poem rehearses much of the traditional material, from Juvenal onwards, with great polish and verve. Some of it is powerful invective, like

Chaste to her husband, frank to all beside,
A teeming mistress but a barren bride.
Men, some to business, some to pleasure take;
But every woman is at heart a rake.

But in the end Pope returns to his old theme of the pathos of beauty: satire is subsumed into a lament for the passing of youth:

See how the world its veterans rewards:
A youth of frolics, an old age of cards. . . .
See, round and round the ghosts of beauty glide,
And haunt the places where their honour died.

The literal meaning is that old dowagers revisit the ballrooms where they were first seduced; but the effect of the music and imagery is one of infinite sadness. It is impossible in the space of this [article] to pursue the subject of anti-feminist satire through the late eighteenth to the twentieth century. The radicals of the Enlightenment and most of the Romantics were pro-feminist, enough for the topic to decline in significance. The consequences of tension between the sexes is explored in the nineteenth century, mainly in regions lying well outside satire. But a later revival of the genre took place in early twentieth-century America, though perhaps that too is now a closed chapter. The special status of women and the special power of the matriarch in the United States have been commented on by sociologists; we need not discuss the causes but must note the literary consequences. If Philip Wylie's invective on 'Mom' in his *Generation of Vipers* deals heavy-handedly with the all-powerful White Goddess figure, the theme receives a classic realistic treatment in the short stories of Ring Lardner, and achieves mythical status in the cartoons and essays of James Thurber, who transforms the Strindbergian sex war into an absurd and touching mock-epic. More recently, there is an exquisitely acid account of the New England wife and mother in one chapter of John Cheever's otherwise undistinguished novel *The Wapshot Chronicle*. Finally there is *Lolita* (1955). A dozen years after the stormy appearance of this book few would still be willing to acclaim Vladimir Nabokov as a great romantic novelist: but of the anti-feminist satire he is certainly a minor master. He attacks the topic of sexuality with the agility and venom of a featherweight boxer: Humbert Humbert's obsession is the starting point for a poetic evocation of an America (who knows whether it is real or not) where the mother, the educationalist and the nymphet reign with the triple majesty of Hecate, goddess of crossroads. For a moment he recaptures the primeval awe out of which this kind of satire arose.

CHAPTER 2

Classic Satire

Satire

The Narrow Scope of Juvenal's *The Sixteen Satires*

Peter Green

In the following article, Peter Green contends that
Roman satirist Juvenal wrote *The Sixteen Satires*
from a very limited viewpoint. According to Green,
Juvenal was essentially a conservative who believed
that the upper class should set good examples and
who detested the newly rich of Roman society because their success made it more difficult for him to
achieve the middle-class status he desired. In his
satires, particularly the Sixth Satire—a famous invective against wealthy women—Juvenal shows that
what angers him most is the breaching of conventions, not the structure or inequality of Roman society. Green is a professor emeritus of classics at the
University of Texas in Austin. His books include
*Alexander to Actium: The Historical Evolution of the
Hellenistic Age* and *The Greco-Persian Wars*. This essay has been excerpted from Green's translation of
Juvenal's *The Sixteen Satires*.

'On the death of Domitian,' the Younger Pliny[1] wrote, with
characteristic candour, 'I reflected that here was a signal
and glorious opportunity to punish guilt, to avenge misfor-
tune, and to bring oneself into notice.' The reader of Juvenal's *Satires* cannot help but feel that their author (who may
have been on bad terms with Pliny) envisaged an identical
programme. Satire I, his manifesto, and probably the latest
composition in the First Book, announces *indignatio* as his

1. Domitian was the emperor of Rome from 81 to 96 A.D. Cruelty and executions marked
his reign, especially in its later years. He was particularly hated by the aristocracy.
Younger Pliny, who was born in either 61 or 62 A.D. and died in 113 A.D., was a Roman ad-
ministrator and author whose private letters depict life during the Roman Empire.

driving motif, and the world at large as his subject-matter:

> All human endeavours, men's prayers,
> Fears, angers, pleasures, joys and pursuits, these make
> The mixed mash of my verse.

But in fact this programme is never carried out. Juvenal writes from a very limited viewpoint, and the traverse of his attack is correspondingly narrow. Throughout his life, so far as we can tell, he never once questioned the social structure or the moral principles of the regime which had treated him so shabbily. (Any crypto-Republicanism one can detect in his work is no more than a reflection of the fashionable Stoic[2] shibboleths current throughout his lifetime.) All that he asked of the Imperial administration was that its rulers should behave according to the dictates of virtue and morality; as for the upper classes, he seems to have hoped for no more from them than that they should set a good public example and avoid activities liable to tarnish their image with the plebs. His approach to any social problem is, basically, one of static conservatism. He may have thought that the client-patron relationship was fundamentally degrading, but he never envisaged its abolition. He attacked wanton cruelty to slaves, but did not query the concept of slavery itself (another characteristically Stoic attitude). His most violent invective, whether borrowed from the common rhetorical stockpot or the fruit of his own obsessions, is reserved for those who, in one way or another, threaten to disrupt the existing pattern of society, to inject some mobility and dynamism into the class-structure. It follows, *a fortiori* ["with greater reason"], that he will display especial animus against those who have robbed him, and his kind, of their chance to achieve what they regard as their birthright *within that framework*. This is one of the main keys to an understanding of the *Satires*.

Satire I is rightly regarded as a programme-piece: in it Juvenal deploys most of the main themes to which he afterwards returns—vapid, cliché-ridden literature and rhetoric; various kinds of social and sexual obnoxiousness; above all, the corrupting power of wealth. But the attack is both calculated and highly selective: in each case there is a special, and revealing, motive behind it. Juvenal's main point about

2. Stoicism is a Greek philosophy that believes wisdom comes through accepting the rule of natural law and living free from passion, joy, grief, and other strong feelings.

mythological platitudes, acute enough in itself, is that they served as a handy refuge for writers anxious to avoid dangerous contemporary issues: that their unreality is due to deliberate escapism. The reader must draw his own conclusions: Juvenal neither attacks the rhetorical system of education *en principe*, nor the civilization which produced it. Instead he works through a cumulative list of significant illustrations. But his main thesis, developed with passionate intensity through the first three books, is (to put it in economic terms) the appalling influence which mobility of income can have on a static class-structure.

CLASS AND CONVENTION

The actual figures whom Juvenal presents on the stage, both here and in subsequent satires, fall into three broad stylized categories. First, and most interesting as a pointer to Juvenal's own preoccupations, there is the decadent aristocrat— of either sex—who has in some way or other betrayed the upper-class code, whose conduct fails to reach those well-defined social and moral standards imposed on the governing classes as a complement to their privileges. This scapegoat figure is accused of many things, from extortion to miscegenation, from outrageous homosexuality to public appearances in the gladiatorial arena: what is common to each case is the *abrogation of responsible behaviour* which it implies. A governing class that lowers its standards and neglects its traditional duties constitutes a positive danger to the social structure over which it is set. This is what lies behind Juvenal's occasional blurring of social and moral criticism, as when the consul who demeans his office by driving his own gig in public is bracketed with forgers and adulterers, while Nero's crimes rise from mere murder to the climactic horror of his appearances on the stage. The rhetorical anticlimax is a device which Juvenal . . . employs to some effect: but it is hard not to feel the real and passionate animus behind examples of this sort. Juvenal flays upper-class shortcomings all the harder because he sees his world in peril: his terror of social change made him treat infringements of accepted manners or conventions on a par with gross major crimes. In a sense his instinct was sound. Collapsing social standards are as sure a sign of eventual upheaval as the ominous drying up of springs and wells which heralds a volcanic eruption. In the famous Sixth Satire against women, what Juvenal really objects to is not so much licentiousness *tout court* ["without qualification"] as the breaching of class and convention. All his examples are chosen from ladies of high society; and what most arouses his wrath against them is that they contract liaisons with *lower-class* persons such as musicians, actors, or gladiators. (One gets the feeling that he would have no particular objection to a little in-group wife-swopping provided it was done discreetly.) These great ladies are several times compared, disadvantageously, to their social inferiors, who bear children instead of having abortions, and would never indulge in such unfeminine pursuits as swordplay or athletics.

Balancing this picture, and in sharply dramatic contrast to it, is that of the wealthy, base-born *parvenu*,[3] a figure whom Juvenal clearly found both sinister and detestable—with good reason, since as a phenomenon he directly threatened Juvenal's own social position, and that of the whole *rentier* [people whose income comes largely from rents] class in Rome. The rise of the freedman class forms one of the most significant elements in the history of the early Empire. These coarse, clever, thrusting ex-slaves, most often of foreign extraction, suffered from none of the crippling conventions and moral beliefs that every upper-class Roman inherited as part of his emotional luggage. What enabled them to amass such gigantic fortunes, and to force their way into positions of immense political power, was by no means only their native ability. They were cashing in on their masters' ignorance of, and contempt for, a world ruled by commerce and industry. Since the middle-class Equestrian Order, to which Juvenal aspired, was mainly a matter of the right property qualification, freedmen and their descendants began to monopolize all the best posts which it offered. It is no accident that Juvenal, in Satire I, draws so blistering a portrait of the Commander of the Praetorian Guard and the Prefect of Egypt. These were the supreme prizes of any Equestrian's career: in Juvenal's poem they are both held by Egyptians—a jumped-up fishhawker called Crispinus, and a Jew, Tiberius Julius Alexander, whose statue, Juvenal suggests, should be used as a public latrine. He is always referring, enviously, to the capital sum of 400,000 sesterces

---

3. *Parvenus* were people who had recently become wealthy but were looked down upon by those whose wealth had long been established.

which was required for admission to the Order. He and his shabby-genteel friends are kept out of the seats reserved for Equestrians while the sons of panders, auctioneers and gladiators are entitled to them. He attacks those who are irresponsible enough to fritter away their capital and become *déclassé*—a charge he also brings against the aristocrats, but for a different reason: since wealth now is the sole criterion of acceptance and power, they are imperilling their position of authority by destroying the *de facto* foundation on which it rests.

JUVENAL'S SHORTCOMING

Yet though Juvenal regarded enough capital to qualify for Equestrian status as the *summum bonum* ["highest good"], he never indicates in any way that he would consider working to obtain it. He vaguely hopes for it as a gift from God, or 'some godlike human', which presumably is a periphrasis for Imperial patronage. Here we hit on a central and vital factor in his attitude to life. Juvenal was a bred-in-the-bone *rentier*, with all the characteristics of his class: contempt for trade, indifference to practical skills, intense political conservatism, with a corresponding fear of change and revolution; abysmal ignorance of, and indifference to, the economic realities governing his existence; a tendency to see all problems, therefore, in over-simplified moral terms, with the application of right conduct to existing authority as a kind of panacea for all ills. His particular dilemma . . . is that he is living by a set of moral and social assumptions that were obsolete before he was born. The only occupations he will recognize are those of the army, the law, and estate-farming. He is as rigidly and imperceptively snobbish about trade as any nineteenth-century rural squire—and with even less justification. As [Gilbert] Highet says,

> Since his ideal is the farm which supports its owner in modest comfort (or the estates which make a man a knight), he does not realize that Italy now lives by imports. And he will not understand that the Greco-Roman world was built up by the efforts of the shrewd, energetic, competent men who made harbours, highways, aqueducts, drainage-systems, and baths; who cleared the forests and set up the trade-routes; who exchanged the products of the far parts of the globe and ventured on innumerable dangerous voyages.

All he can see in the immense commercial activity of his day is a frantic scrambling after quick profits, stupid luxuries, or wheat to keep the rabble quiet. He is ready to admire Trajan's splendid new harbour at Ostia, but the socially inferior men who built and planned it elicit nothing from him but a quick, dismissive gibe about making money out of privy-contracts—'These are such men as Fortune, by way of a joke,/ Will sometimes raise from the gutter and make Top People.' His ideal is not so far from that of Naevolus, the ageing homosexual gigolo: a small country home bestowed by some wealthy patron; 'a nice little nest-egg at interest/ In gilt-edged stock'; a life of cultivated idleness, the Victorian 'genteel sufficiency'. 'What can I do in Rome?' cries Juvenal's friend Umbricius, in a famous and much-quoted section of Satire III; and the reader is so carried away by the rhetorical brilliance of the passage that it never occurs to him to answer, briefly: 'A useful job of work.' Nor, indeed, does it occur to Juvenal.

PARALLELS TO CHARLES DICKENS

It is sometimes said that Juvenal is a very modern figure, and this is true; but in ways he is far more like a nineteenth-century phenomenon such as Dickens. Indeed, it could be argued, without stretching the paradox too far, that George Orwell's essay on Dickens is the most illuminating introduction to Juvenal in existence. The social parallels are so numerous and striking that they cannot be ignored. Again and again it might be the Roman poet rather than the English novelist that Orwell is analysing. Juvenal, like Dickens, 'displays no consciousness that the *structure* of society can be changed.' Like Dickens again, he lived in 'a city of consumers, of people who are deeply civilized but not primarily useful.' He too records 'pretentious meals and inconvenient houses, when the slavey drudging fourteen hours a day in the basement kitchen was something too normal to be noticed.' He too 'knows very little about the way things really happen. . . . As soon as he has to deal with trade, finance, industry or politics he takes refuge in vagueness, or satire.' He too sees revolution as a monster, and is acutely aware of the irrational bloodlust and opportunism of the mob. . . . He too has a special compassion for children: like Dickens he attacks bad education without proposing a better alternative. His xenophobia may be closer to Thackeray: but what he shares with Dickens more than any of Dickens' own contemporaries—and for much the same reasons—is that special horror of slums and poverty, that ignorance of, and distaste for, the urban proletariat which stand high among 'the special prejudices of the shabby genteel'. Like Dickens, he frowns—as we have seen—on social miscegenation: he objects to Eppia running off with her ugly gladiator for exactly the same reason that Dickens objects to Uriah Heep's passion for Agnes Wicklow. He too is a caricaturist; and as we know, it is fatal when a caricaturist sees too much. He too (like every urban Roman of his age) was 'out of contact with agriculture and politically impotent'. He too 'only succeeds with [the landowning-military-bureaucratic] class when he depicts them as mental defectives.' He too (and this is both his strength and his weakness as a satirist) in the last resort 'sees the world as a middle-class world, and everything outside these limits is either laughable or slightly wicked.'

Jonathan Swift's Satire of Travel Epics in *Gulliver's Travels*

Michael Seidel

Michael Seidel explains in the following article the ways in which Jonathan Swift's novel *Gulliver's Travels* serves as a satire of travel literature. According to Seidel, Swift used the adventures of Lemuel Gulliver to mock the experiences related in travel narratives popular in the eighteenth century. Unlike the heroes of traditional travel literature, Gulliver loses his sense of self and consequently his desire to return home. Gulliver's identity becomes skewed because he finds his status, both physically and socially, varying in every country he reaches. By the time he returns home after visiting so many unusual lands and people, Gulliver is barely able to relate to fellow humans. When his story concludes, Gulliver has become a lunatic whose compulsion to continue traveling has left him uncomfortable in his homeland, if not his own body. Seidel is a professor of English and comparative literature at Columbia University and the author of *Epic Geography: James Joyce's Ulysses, Robinson Crusoe: Island Myths and the Novel*, and *Satiric Inheritance: Rabelais to Sterne*, the source of the following selection.

Hugh Kenner has written an engaging short book called *The Counterfeiters*, which has an apt subtitle, *an Historical Comedy*. Kenner's subtitle suggests a particular vision of literary process tied to a set of preoccupations that began in the later seventeenth century and characterized "the great artists of an astonishing half-century, 1690–1740."

We call them satirists, they called themselves (having no bet-

Excerpted from *Satiric Inheritance: Rabelais to Sterne* by Michael Seidel (Princeton, NJ: Princeton University Press, 1979). Copyright © 1979 by Michael Seidel. Reprinted with permission.

ter word) satirists; they were, Swift and Pope, great realists, great modernists. They had responded, we are going to see, to a new definition of man, proper to the new universe of empirical fact, which definition still obtains because we are still in that universe. They transmuted, to the point of destruction, the old ritual genres, tragedy, comedy, epic, which were proper to an older universe.

Counterfeit is revision with a vengeance—a sly vengeance. The "Historical Comedy" of Kenner's subtitle is itself the counterfeiting of literary history, the comic reproduction or imitation that records and debases at the same time. For the satirist the world of empirical fact works as it does for the counterfeiter: "retaining its contours, altering its nature." Satirists see a double potential in all recorded action, which reflects a measure of generic displacement or duplicity. Gulliver is a travelling man, *homo viator*, but he is also a decentered or counterfeit hero. He shares a remembered generic destiny with sorts as variable as Odysseus and Robinson Crusoe. In parodying the idea of the nationally displaced hero, Swift addresses the epic of his time, the epic of territorial exploration and expansion in unknown continents and seas of the world. The spaces of the *Travels* are suspiciously extreme: the first and last books are set beyond *terra australis incognita* in a satirical underworld of sorts (or at least "down under"); the second adventure occurs near or about the mythical Northwest Passage (the traditional land of fallen giants); and the third adventure is set in the uncharted waters of the oriental Pacific.

PARODYING THE TRAVEL NARRATIVE

The conjunction of epic and travel literature can be traced back to the Greek geographer Strabo, who based a good part of his writings on the presumed accuracy of the Homeric Mediterranean adventures. Of course the counterassumption formed the ironic basis for [Greek satirist] Lucian's Homeric parody in the *True History*. Those predisposed to skepticism always treat travel literature in as antagonistic a manner as they treat heroic marvels. Thus Voltaire writes of historical methodology in his *Philosophical Dictionary:* "When Herodotus relates what he was told by the barbarians among whom he traveled, he relates nonsense; but most of our travelers do the same." And although Gulliver is hardly one to trust, he voices a similar sentiment after his rescue from Brobdingnag:

I thought we were already overstocked with Books of Travels: That nothing could now pass which was not extraordinary; wherein I doubted, some Authors less consulted Truth than their own Vanity or Interest, or the Diversion of ignorant Readers. That my Story could contain little besides common Events, without those ornamental Descriptions of strange Plants, Trees, Birds, and other Animals; or the barbarous Customs and Idolatry of savage People, with which most Writers abound. However, I thanked him for his good Opinion, and promised to take the Matter into my Thoughts.

That Gulliver demurs is both a joke and a commentary upon the state of the art. Swift's friend Frances Hutcheson offers some observations about the status of travel literature in 1726, the same year Swift published the *Travels*.

A Late Ingenious Author . . . has justly observ'd the Absurdity of the *monstrous Taste*, which has possess'd both the *Readers* and *Writers* of *Travels*. They scarce give us any Account of the *natural Affections, the Familys, Associations, Friendships, Clans*, of the *Indians;* and as rarely do they mention their Abhorrence of *Treachery* among themselves; their *Proneness* to mutual Aid, and to the Defence of their several *States;* their Contempt of Death in defence of their Country, or upon points of *Honour.* "These are but *common-Storys*—No need to travel to the *Indies* for what we see in Europe every Day." The Entertainment therefore in these ingenious Studys consists chiefly in exciting *Horror*, and making Men *Stare*. The ordinary Employment of the Bulk of the *Indians* in support of their Wives and Offspring, or Relations, has nothing of the *Prodigious*. But a *Human Sacrifice*, a Feast upon Enemys Carcases, can raise an Horror and Admiration of the wondrous Barbarity of *Indians*, in Nations no strangers to the *Massacre at Paris*, the *Irish Rebellion*, or the Journals of the *Inquisition*. These they behold with religious Veneration; but the *Indian Sacrifices*, flowing from a like Perversion of *Humanity* by *Superstition*, raise the highest Abhorrence and Amazement. What is most suprizing in these Studys is the wondrous *Credulity* of some Gentlemen, of great Pretensions in other matters to Caution of Assent, for these *marvellous Memoirs* of Monks, Fryars, Sea-Captains, Pyrites; and for the *Historys, Annals, Chronologys*, receiv'd by Oral Tradition, or Hieroglyphicks.

Hutcheson's complaint is one that had received even more eloquent expression in [Michel de] Montaigne's famous essay "Of Cannibals." Swift's Gulliver arrives as a satiric corrective for such complaints. But as is often the case with satire, it exacerbates before it amends. Try as he might to keep his record within the bounds of mundane description, the extravagances of the travel genre force poor Gulliver to the extraordinary. Each voyage begins with a probable des-

tination and ends with an improbable place. Swift's strategy
is primarily Lucianic, but he borrows from travels as remote
as Sir Thomas More's *Utopia*, [François] Rabelais' later
Northwest Passage books, Cyrano de Bergerac's atmospheric
travel histories, even [Daniel] Defoe's allegorical lunar journey, *The Consolidator.*

THE UNSETTLED TERRITORY OF *GULLIVER'S TRAVELS*

The satiric traveller is an antithetical figure. As he "moves
out," he understands less. In serious travel literature, the
home order or the normative order is the basis of measured value so that in the voyage out there is both a psychological and intellectual pressure to move back in, to ac-
climate, familiarize, adjust, and in one way or another
come home. As a narrative or strategic promise, home-
coming is the final falling into place of travel literature—no
voyager, imagined or actual, leaves home with the *intent* of
permanent exile. Perhaps this is why the traditional utopia
or *no place* is usually so alien and extreme. Utopia is home
only for antithetical natures.

An essential strategy in the satiric or parodic travel narrative is the confusion of the "no place" with the "home place."
Primitive forms such as the "Antipodes" satire, where the
utopian realm is at geographical and cultural odds with the
homeland (that is turned upside down), serve as ready examples of the process in outline, and there are antipodal elements in all of the books of *Gulliver's Travels.* But the more
complex satiric parodies of travel narrative work with more
subtle means of psychological and spatial unsettlement. In
Swift's *Travels*, the most unsettled place is the mental terri-
tory of the traveller. Gulliver loses the will to go home because his sense of himself as a homebody deteriorates—he
prefers geographical displacement. Even at home he seeks
the stable rather than the house. Like Achilles, he can talk to
horses, but unlike Achilles, he gains no glory from doing so.

At the end of his travels Gulliver is a figure without a
ground. All of his life he has shared a characteristic feature
of the wanderer, "an insatiable Desire of seeing foreign
Countries," but that desire is finally subverted by an antagonism to the place of origin. The original wanderer, Odysseus,
is sanctioned in his wanderlust partly because of his great
desire to return. Only after he reestablishes himself as a native force do the post-Homeric legends of his further voyages

begin, the most famous of which is recorded in Dante's *Inferno*. Significantly, for Dante the centrifugal spirit is a kind of motion sickness, and Ulysses is the tragic version of the perpetually exiled traveller. Hell's exile is perhaps worse than Gulliver's home stable because the denied home is the promised Earthly Paradise.

In the *True History*, Lucian begins his satiric subversion of the homing epic by insisting that his narrator make the same tragic step that Dante was later to record—the step beyond the Pillars of Hercules into unknown waters. Lucian abandons the depth of epic values for the abnormal range of parodic displacement. Similarly, Swift works to undermine the measure of the home place by making Gulliver increasingly unsure of what normative measure means. In the initial voyages, accident makes him a monster or a *lusus naturae*. Eventually he succeeds in distorting his own lineaments by mad devise. His homing instinct is shapeless because by the end he has no shape that he wants to call his own. Even earlier in his *Travels*, after the Brobdingnagian adventure, he had realized that proportion was a relative thing, but his realization made it no easier for him to contemplate his altered physical status: "I could never endure to look in a Glass after mine Eyes had been accustomed to such prodigious Objects; because the Comparison gave me so despicable a Conceit of my self." When at the end of the *Travels* he returns home to a place where he would rather not be and to a place that would probably prefer not to have him, he again looks in the mirror, this time with a thought to self-accommodation: "to behold my Figure often in a Glass, and thus if possible habituate my self by Time to tolerate the Sight of a human Creature." Satiric travel is schizophrenic, and Gulliver loses formal integrity when his spatial and proportionate insecurity befuddles his home image. After Brobdingnag all England seems Lilliputian to Gulliver (which, by satiric analogy, it was). He notes that until he can readjust, his family "concluded I had lost my Wits." Later, when first introduced to the estate of the Horse of Quality in Houyhnhnmland, Gulliver reaches the same conclusion about himself: "I feared my Brain was disturbed by my Sufferings and Misfortunes." Gulliver has been set up. His final madness is the satiric concentration of displacement in the homeless body and soul of the traveller.

In Lilliput Gulliver's stature gave him the name of moun-

tain and allowed him the role of human arch. To the Blefus-
cans he was a veritable Leviathan. In Brobdingnag he is
thought to be a species of weasel, toad, spider, or unnamed
vermin: a piece of clockwork; perhaps even "an Embrio, or
abortive Birth." The kitchen clerk's monkey gives him "good
Reason to believe that he took me for a young one of his own
Species," something Gulliver has occasion to remember
when he is later mounted by a female Yahoo in Houyhnhnmland. At the end of his fourth voyage his wife embraces him
at home, and Swift's *homo viator* faints dead away. The smell
of his faithful Penelope is alien to his "perfected" nose. Earlier Gulliver's wife protested that the kind of voyaging Gulliver subjects himself to makes torture out of readjustment.
She wants no more of unsettled behavior: "But my Wife
protested I should never go to Sea any more; although my
evil Destiny so ordered, that she had not Power to hinder
me." For Gulliver's wife, voyaging is the equivalent of alien-
ated affection, and it is a kind of madness constantly to test
one's powers of readjustment. In a narrative sense, to send
Gulliver out over and over again is to insure that he loses the
capacity to return whole.

THE BEHAVIOR OF OTHER TRAVELLERS

Satiric travels are something of an overextension, and at the
end of his *Travels* Gulliver is like the restless author of *A
Tale of A Tub:* once maddened by surfaces, his depths become lunatic. The *Tale*'s author is no more a homecomer
than is Gulliver.

> For in *Writing,* it is as in *Travelling:* If a Man is in haste to be
> at home, (which I acknowledge to be none of my Case, hav-
> ing never so little Business, as when I am there) if his *Horse*
> be tired with long Riding, and ill Ways, or be naturally a Jade,
> I advise him clearly to make the straitest and the commonest
> Road, be it ever so dirty; But, then surely, we must own such
> a Man to be a scurvy Companion at best; He *spatters* himself
> and his Fellow-Travellers at every Step: All their Thoughts,
> and Wishes, and Conversation turn entirely upon the Subject
> of their Journey's End; and at every Splash, and Plunge, and
> Stumble, they heartily wish one another the Devil.

The author of the *Tale* views the very notion of the cen-
tripetal fiction as singleminded: he prefers the range and
pace of modernity. But to be in perpetual motion is to see too
much of the surface of things, to start by fits and to end by
starts. When Gulliver's travels are over, he begins them

again by recording them. Here, too, he feels betrayed by the home front. He protests that cuts have been made in his text after its release to an editor. As a writer, just as a traveller,

---

REACTIONS TO THE FINAL VOYAGE

The final voyage of Jonathan Swift's Gulliver's Travels, *where the title character encounters the repugnant Yahoos (humans), sparked considerable reaction by learned authors of the time. Literary critic and historian Ernest Tuveson shows how Gulliver's voyage was considered both a powerful yet unpleasant satire.*

It is of course the last Voyage that has been most responsible for the Swift legend, for the mixture of admiration, fear, and hatred with which Swift's name is associated. The hysterical reactions to the yahoos have perhaps no counterpart among responses to any other literary work. There was some consolation in the once widely believed notion that what Sir Edmund Gosse called "the awful satire of the Yahoos" was the "horrible satisfaction of disease," the product of "a brain not wholly under control." [William Makepeace] Thackeray's *cri de coeur* against the yahoos suggests that, whether Swift's intellect was under control or not, Thackeray's own was not in perfect order. "What had this man done? What secret remorse was rankling at his heart, what fever was boiling in him, that he should see all the world blood-shot?" Yet Swift could have retorted that [Thackeray's] *Vanity Fair*, even its title, gives support to his own picture of the degeneracy of human nature. The shrillness of these outbursts, even from writers as normally placid as Sir Walter Scott, suggests that the satire has touched them in a special way. Swift has forced them to see what appears to be their own image, but horribly distorted in the mirror: they look for any means of escape from that vision, for a mirror reflects the truth. Swift might well have taken the attacks, even in his own time, as the best proof that he had indeed accomplished the seemingly impossible—to make the world really feel the lash of satire. [Alexander] Pope called Swift an "Avenging Angel of wrath," and asserted that he would make the "wretched pityful creatures of this world" "*Eat your Book*, which you have made as bitter a pill for them as possible"; it was indeed Swift's achievement to realize this, the ancient goal of strong satire.

Ernest Tuveson, "Swift: The View from Within the Satire." From H. James Jensen and Malvin R. Zirker Jr., eds., *The Satirist's Art*. Bloomington: Indiana University Press, 1972.

he would have gone on further if he could. In another sense, his writing simply prolongs the record of his madness. Satire's wanderings do not rest upon terra firma. Gulliver begins his voyaging as a ship's surgeon whose mind is something less than surgical. At the end he is captain, and his ship is served by one Dr. Purefoy. Pure faith is satiric gullibility, and the satiric motion appears to be starting all over again. By navigating through the world, Purefoy will certainly lose the purity and the faith his name is heir to.

The displaced hero courts one or another form of madness. Insecure at home, Hamlet makes a fool of himself; sterile in his capacity as a farmer, Don Quixote travels in circles as a lunatic Hidalgo [Spanish knight or noble]; parasitical by design, Rameau's nephew [in Denis Dident's *Rameau's Nephew*] is frenetic for his supper. Homelessness is maddening. What makes *Gulliver's Travels* even more intriguing in this respect is that, as in Swift's own *Tale of A Tub* or in [Fyodor] Dostoevsky's *Notes from Underground* or in [Vladimir] Nabakov's *Pale Fire*, the madman is given just enough presence of mind to record the process of his own lunacy.

THE EXPERIENCES OF A MADMAN

When Swift added the letter from Gulliver to his cousin Sympson to the 1735 edition of the *Travels*, he further complicated the problem. How can an author be trusted who rants as does Gulliver to his slightly embarrassed cousin and editor? What generates his values? The tone of the letter makes no sense until we have read the entire *Travels*. If we do read the *Travels* through (and thereby understand the prefixed letter), we are forced to conclude that even the earlier voyages are being relayed from the perspective of a madman whose sense of an audience is no more secure than his grasp on his reason. In the 1735 edition, Gulliver not only gives us an inkling of the way his condition can be held against him but of the way Swift holds a crazed Gulliver against the entire genre of travel literature: "If the Censure of *Yahoos* could any Way affect me, I should have great Reason to complain, that some of them are so bold as to think my Book of Travels a meer Fiction out of mine Brain; and have gone so far as to drop Hints, that the *Houyhnhnms* and *Yahoos* have no more Existence than the Inhabitants of *Utopia*."

That a madman should take so offended a tone comports with the earlier Swiftian notion from the *Tale of A Tub* that the brain's fancies have the power to leap astride reason. Of course Gulliver could point to ocular proof—the miniature cows from Lilliput or the wasp stings from Brobdingnag. But perhaps these are figments of his imagination as well. Further, he tells the professor at Lagado of his visits to the Kingdom of Tribnia (Britain) called Langden (England), and since he makes no claims to being the only European to have visited these territories, we could conclude that all his travels are but encoded versions of home as experienced by a madman. Lunacy means to be mentally far away no matter where one's body is, a state admittedly reached by Gulliver at the end of his travels. The loss of powers that enables a narrator to discriminate, concentrate, and penetrate becomes part of the degenerative representation of Swift's satiric fiction. Gulliver's status as a truth teller—a man possessed by imagined truths—is a compromised status. Cousin Sympson boasts (presumably by way of relation, since he is sheepish in most regards) that Gulliver "was so distinguished for his Veracity, that it became a Sort of Proverb among his Neighbours at *Redriff* when any one affirmed a Thing, to say, it was as true as if Mr. *Gulliver* had spoke it." Somehow this remark by Sympson registers more loyalty than conviction.

Given free reign at home, the horse-mimicking Gulliver is likely to run away with himself. By his own testimony he worries that his manuscript has been tampered with, he offers corrections, he prepares supplementary texts detailing a more fully documented madness. Apparently the *Travels* as we have them are but the ur-text of a travelling fancy. Gulliver is similar to the author of the *Tale* who has things in store for posterity. In fact, a quick glance at the proposed oeuvre of the *Tale*'s author momentarily raises the prospect that Swift's two lunatics share satiric experiences. Of the promised titles, two read: "*A Description of the Kingdom of* Absurdities" and "*A Voyage into* England, *by a Person of Quality in* Terra Australia incognita, *translated from the Original.*" *Gulliver's Travels* fulfills a part of the *Tale*'s promise: absurdity is figured in satiric ethnocentricity, and a native of Australia might in one sense be a Hottentot but in another is a would-be Houyhnhnm.

Voltaire's *Candide* Debunks the Romanticized World

George R. Havens

In the following excerpt from his introduction to *Candide*, George R. Havens relates some of the inspirations for and targets of Voltaire's satire. *Candide* ironically flouts the conventions of seventeenth-century French novels, which featured long-separated lovers, pirates, shipwrecks, and other unrealistic adventures. Voltaire wished to portray the world as it was, not create a romanticized ideal where everything worked out for the best. Related to his criticism of an edenic world, Voltaire also satirizes religion, because he scorned the Catholic Church's hypocrisy in claiming all are brothers while its adherents support war, practice slavery, and burn heretics. In addition, Voltaire targets greed, cruelty, false flattery, and other human failings. However, Havens concludes that while *Candide* may be one-sided in its attacks, Voltaire is not entirely pessimistic. The ultimate message of *Candide* seems to suggest that people should work and accomplish what they can in the face of human wickedness. Havens is the author of several books on Voltaire and French literature, including *Selections from Voltaire* and *Jean-Jacques Rousseau*.

The philosophy of Optimism, Leibnitz, Pope, the earthquake at Lisbon, Jean-Jacques Rousseau and the discussion over Providence, *Scarmentado*, the *Essai sur les Mœurs*,[1] all played

1. German philosopher and mathematician Gottfried Wilhelm Leibnitz was the first person to propose the philosophy of Optimism, which states that ours is the best of all possible worlds. The Lisbon earthquake occurred in 1755. It was followed by a tidal wave and fire, all of which combined to destroy much of the city. French philosopher Rousseau, who believed in Optimism, and Voltaire disagreed in a number of writings on the relationship between Providence and evil. *Scarmentado* and *Essai sur les Mœurs* are other works by Voltaire.

prominent parts in furnishing inspiration or material for *Candide*. All through the novel numberless incidents can be directly traced to one or another of these sources. There is still another important influence, however, which determined the very form and framework in which the novel was composed. When Voltaire sat down to write this novel, the main characteristics of his rapidly-moving plot were ready to his hand. He had only to draw upon the conventionalities of the popular novels of adventure and thwarted love and treat ironically what his predecessors had written seriously. Thus his satire falls not only upon his philosophical opponents, his numerous personal enemies, and upon human frailty, ferocity, and wickedness in general, but also upon the unreality and exaggeration of popular romance throughout the seventeenth and eighteenth centuries down to the time of the composition of *Candide* itself.

THE ROMANTIC VISION

In the seventeenth century two main tendencies in the French novels of the time early revealed themselves, corresponding to the two ever-divergent characteristics of the human mind in all ages, the idealistic and the realistic. Thus the pastoral romance of Honoré d'Urfé, *L'Astrée* (1607–1627), under the guise of shepherds and shepherdesses, represented the *préciosité*, the high-flown sentiments, and the somewhat affected language which as ideals at least were supplanting in aristocratic circles the blunt grossness of the troubled period of civil war immediately preceding. Like the love-sick hero Céladon separated from his beloved Astrée, Candide too after leaving El Dorado will carve the name of his absent sweetheart Cunégonde on the bark of trees, but in the former case the author is serious, in the latter satirical. . . . Shipwrecks, kidnappings by rival suitors, the incursions of corsairs and pirates, recognition scenes in which long-separated characters are suddenly and unexpectedly reunited, furnish the regular stock in trade of these and many later novels. These very same elements reappear satirically in *Candide*. Such in brief was the idealistic novel of the seventeenth century. It was early satirized in realistic *bourgeois* novels like [Charles] Sorel's *Francion* (1622) and *Le Berger extravagant* (1627–1628), [Paul] Scarron's *Roman comique* (1651–1657), and [Antoine] Furetière's *Roman bourgeois* (1665). The critic [Nicolas] Boileau in a brief, witty dialogue,

Les Héros de roman, composed in 1665, but not printed until 1688, likewise effectively poked fun at the same excesses. In attitude at least, if not in manner, Voltaire in *Candide* continues this tradition of matter-of-fact common sense and *terre à terre* realism. Perhaps even [Miguel] Cervantes's *Don Quijote* (1605–1615), of which Voltaire had in his library the Spanish original as well as a French translation, was not entirely without influence in this connection, but, if so, it constituted only one more impulse in the direction he was naturally inclined to follow.

In the eighteenth century the novels of D'Urfé, Gomberville, La Calprenède, and Mlle de Scudéry continued to be popular. They were not killed off by the satire of Sorel, Scarron, Furetière, or Boileau. All but Gomberville were represented in the library of Voltaire himself. Of D'Urfé's *Astrée* Lenglet du Fresnoy, a contemporary authority, wrote in 1734: "Sa réputation se soutient toujours depuis plus d'un siècle." ["Its reputation has always been supported for more than one century."] Other novelists continued the tradition of exaggerated fiction and adventure. Although the Abbé Prévost is today remembered for the classic simplicity of his *Manon Lescaut* (1731), his contemporaries thought especially of the now nearly forgotten *Mémoires et Aventures d'un homme de qualité* (1728–1731), of *Cléveland, fils naturel de Cromwell* (1731–1739), of *Le Doyen de Killerine* (1736–1740), or of *L'Histoire d'une Grecque moderne* (1740), filled with "torrents of tears," swooning heroines, unexpected recognition scenes, somber narratives of violent death by the duelist's sword, journeys from country to country, even on occasion amongst the "communistic" savages of America who in this communism somewhat resemble the inhabitants of El Dorado in *Candide*. Other novelists less well known than Prévost mixed similar ingredients and enjoyed wide popularity. No wonder Voltaire in his *Siècle de Louis XIV* (1751) decried "tour ces romans dont la France a été et est encore inondée" ["All these books that

Voltaire

France had in the summer and with which they are still in-undated"] and called them "des productions d'esprits faibles qui écrivent avec facilité des choses indignes d'être lues par les esprits solides." ["These products of weak spirits who write easily of unworthy things to be read by solid spirits."] This is of course an excessive statement which takes no account of the occasional work of genius already in process of raising the novel in France to a major *genre,* but it was true of a great mass of popular productions and explains the plot of *Candide* and one whole side of its satire. Voltaire too wanted to try his hand at laughing the romantic novel of adventure out of court.

Still another tradition lay behind him. Many novels of travel had been used as vehicles for ideas. It was safer in an age of censorship to present under the guise of fiction criti-cism of contemporary society or admiration for the idealized manners and customs of primitive peoples of far-off lands. All sorts of extraordinary and imaginary voyages, as well as occasional real voyages, fulfilled this function as *romans philosophiques.* [Gabriel de] Foigny's *La terre australe con-nue* or *Les Aventures de Jacques Sadeur* (1676), Tissot de Pa-tot's *Voyages et Aventures de Jacques Massé* (1710), and De-nis Vairasse's *Histoire des Sévarambes* (1677–1679) are three of the most important. Even the *Relations* of Jesuit mission-aries furnished similar material. Garcilaso de la Vega's *His-toire des Yncas, Roys du Pérou,* had appeared in French translation in 1633 and was several times reprinted during the eighteenth century. These works along with Sir Walter Raleigh's *Discoverie of Guiana,* first published at the end of the sixteenth century, but available in a French translation of 1722, are especially significant here as the main sources of the details of Voltaire's Utopia which as the mythical El Dorado furnished a foil to the realistic horrors of the rest of Candide's world. Add to these such works as [François de] Fénelon's *Télémaque* (1699), Montesquieu's *Lettres persanes* (1721), Le Sage's picaresque *Gil Blas* (1715–1735), to which Candide bears interesting resemblances, and numerous *con-tes philosophiques,* now forgotten but indicative of the great popularity of this rising *genre,* and we can more easily un-derstand why Voltaire even in his old age should feel that here was a vehicle for his ideas too important to neglect. Furnishing a marvelous synthesis both of his own ideas and of what had gone before him, Voltaire did not so much cre-ate, he surpassed. . . .

Voltaire's View of Reality

Voltaire . . . is prodigal of his wealth of resources. In sentence after sentence his ready irony flashes out in potent thrusts at human foibles or wickedness or at the ridiculousness or the cruelty of human institutions. Thus, brief as it is, *Candide* is an extraordinarily complete picture of what human life is, but ought not to be. It is at once the broadest of indictments and by implication a whole program of reform.

Pride of rank appears in German insistence upon *quartiers* of noble birth or the Baron's persistent refusal to consent to Candide's marriage with Cunégonde. Similarly the Governor of Buenos Ayres, Don Fernando d'Ibaraa y Figueora y Mascarenes y Lampourdos y Souza, struts his brief moment across the stage with a haughtiness befitting his wealth of sonorous names. Court flattery is deftly hit in a quick reference to laughter evoked by the jokes of the Westphalian Baron of Thunder-ten-tronckh. The dignity of the Baroness's three hundred plump pounds wins a sentence from Voltaire. Private enemies, Père Croust, [Élie-Catherine] Fréron, Maupertuis, the *Journal de Trévoux,* the Dutch publisher Van Düren, the Jesuits, are among those who feel the sting of his satire in allusions now obscure to the general reader but full of reality when they were written.

More important is Voltaire's attack upon human greed for gold and precious stones implied when Candide and Cacambo pick up the dust and pebbles of El Dorado. Avarice and trickery appear in the ship captain Vanderdendur (who is the Van Düren mentioned above), as he makes away with the bulk of Candide's wealth. There is the heartless ingratitude of the sailor who indifferently watches his rescuer, the Anabaptist Jacques, while the sea sweeps him overboard to death. The Protestant minister in Holland attacks the Pope instead of practicing charity. Gambling and cheating at cards feature Candide's visit to the salon of Mme de Parolignac as her victims endeavor by trickery to "réparer les cruautés du sort." ["Repair the cruelties of chance."] There are corsairs and pirates on the Mediterranean and on the high seas. No wonder that at the spectacle of so much wickedness Candide bursts out: "Croyez-vous . . . que les hommes se soient toujours mutuellement massacrés, comme ils font aujourd'hui, qu'ils aient toujours été menteurs, fourbes, perfides, ingrats, brigands, faibles, volages, lâches, envieux, gourmands, ivrognes, avares, ambitieux, sanguinaires, calomniateurs, débauchés, fanatiques, hypocrites et sots?" ["Do you think . . . that men have always massacred each other as they do today, and that they have always been liars, cheaters, traitors, ingrates, brigands, weaklings, deserters, cowards, enviers, gluttons, drunks, misers, profiteers, predators, slanderers, perverts, fanatics, hypocrites, and morons?"]

But Voltaire does not limit himself to attacking individual human foibles or wickedness. More dangerous still are the manifestations of ferocity or cruelty in what have become established institutions of society. Judges and courts are as indifferent to justice in Surinam as in England or Paris. Worst of all no doubt is that murder on a large scale which is called war. The Bulgars and the Abars typify the Prussians and the French then in the midst of the Seven Years' War. All the "heroic butchery" of battle, the burning, pillaging, and ravishing of men amuck with primeval savagery, are sketched by Voltaire in a few swift sentences which are only the more effective because of their skillful brevity. Military drill and discipline witnessed from the palace windows of Potsdam receive their due share of the author's cutting irony. Among the anomalies which constantly called forth Voltaire's scorn was the spectacle of the Church blessing war. On both sides of the lines *Te Deum* was being said, thanksgiving for victory or prayer to ward off defeat. Christianity, which professed human brotherhood, accepted and supported war, the negation of all its moral and ethical ideals. So-called Christian nations actually furnished arms to the Moors against other Christians. There is irony in the fact that a Jesuit officer could be at the same time Colonel and Priest. International law legalizes the violation of human rights. The Church itself has its Inquisition and burns heretics in a so-called Act of Faith, Auto-da-fé, while ladies witness the ceremony and eat refreshments. Christians are held in slavery by the Moors. The former in turn practice negro slavery and treat their slaves with a cruelty which no civilization should countenance. The Jesuits in Paraguay rule with complete indifference to the rights and welfare of their native subjects. Galley slaves toil over their oars beneath the lash of their cruel overseers.

A PRACTICAL SOLUTION

Human beliefs, social classes, music, art and literature, France, Germany, Italy, Spain, Portugal, America, Turkey, the scourges of disease and catastrophe, all are the objects of satire from Voltaire's pen. The picture is complete, too complete even for enumeration in brief space. Any careful reader of *Candide* could fill in numerous details here omitted.

At first sight so black a picture may seem the work of a confirmed pessimist who looks upon humanity with despairing eyes. Not so, however. Of course, *Candide* is intentionally one-sided. No carefully balanced account of good and evil could shock mankind into revolt. Only the unremitting hammering of Voltaire's attack could penetrate the armor of complacency and indifference with which humanity is but too well fortified. Stupid indeed and smug must he be, however, who can read *Candide* without something of the moral jolt intended by its author. Once shaken from acceptance of long existing evils, humanity may then proceed to "cultivate its garden." Voltaire has pointed out the weeds. There is work to be done. Let every one bear a hand. This is the counsel of *Candide,* not a counsel of despair, of pessimism, and defeat. It is a counsel of courage, of work, of accomplishment, in the face of clear-seeing recognition of human wickedness and misery. Voltaire's philosophy is eminently practical.

Jane Austen's *Northanger Abbey* Is a Satire of Sentimental Novels

Amy Elizabeth Smith

Jane Austen's novel *Northanger Abbey* is often considered a satire of the Gothic novels that were popular in the late eighteenth century. In the following selection, Amy Elizabeth Smith contends that Austen is also satirizing another genre, the sentimental novel. According to Smith, Austen's depiction of Catherine Morland, the heroine of *Northanger Abbey*, parodies the portrayal of the title characters in sentimental novels such as *Julia* and *Louisa*. In these works, the heroines are exceptionally accomplished, surrounded by tragedies and scheming, and attract the attention of almost everyone around them. By contrast, argues Smith, Austen's heroine is unexceptional in abilities as well as background. In addition, Catherine Morland's pragmatism serves to spoof the overwrought emotions of the sentimental novel heroines. Smith concludes that understanding the ways in which Austen satirizes sentimental novels provides a more complete context to *Northanger Abbey*. Smith is an assistant professor of English at the University of the Pacific in Stockton, California.

Jane Austen's *Northanger Abbey* (written 1797–98; published 1818) is both a witty and sympathetic burlesque of the popular late eighteenth century gothic genre. Interest in the gothic element of the novel has, however, often obscured the other important target of Austen's satire—the sentimental novel. Her parodies of such sentimental authors as Fanny

From "'Julias and Louisas': Austen's *Northanger Abbey* and the Sentimental Novel," by Amy Elizabeth Smith, *English Language Notes*, September 1992. Copyright © 1992 by *English Language Notes*. Reprinted with permission.

Burney and Charlotte Smith, whose works remain in print, are easy to distinguish. But what of the many "inferior imitations" of Burney's fiction? Austen certainly would have been familiar with more than the few late eighteenth century novels still considered worth reading in the 1990s, but what novels these might have been has remained unclear. In Chapter VI of *Northanger Abbey* one finds the names of the seven "horrid" gothic novels, but Austen supplies no convenient list of minor sentimental fiction.

In Chapter XIV, however, is a passage that may illuminate more clearly the relationship between Austen's burlesque and the minor sentimental novel. Henry Tilney, who tells Catherine Morland that he has read "hundreds and hundreds" of novels, warns her not to attempt to compete with him "in a knowledge of Julias and Louisas." This passage is not annotated in Chapman's standard edition of Austen or in most other recent editions, and those editors who do note it read the passage as a general reference to common heroines' names. In 1790, however, when Austen was 14 and at work on her humorous burlesque juvenilia, two novels were published bearing these names as titles—*Julia,* by Helen Maria Williams, and *Louisa,* by Elizabeth Hervey. While the reference may encompass more than just these two novels, an examination of each reveals a number of parallels, both minor and significant, to elements of plot and characterization burlesqued by Austen in *Northanger Abbey;* no other "Julia" or "Louisa" novel of the period examined for this study contains even half as many parallels.

A COMPARISON OF PLOTS AND HEROINES

The plots of both novels can be outlined quickly. In *Julia,* Williams presents a stern moral picture of "the fatal effects which may arise from the unrestrained indulgence of the passion of love." The beautiful friendship between Julia and her cousin Charlotte is threatened when the latter's intended, Frederick Seymour, falls desperately in love with Julia. Janet Todd notes that "interestingly, however, it is the man rather than the woman who dies under the strain." The heroine remains virtuous, and her friendship with Charlotte is restored. Mrs. Hervey's *Louisa* is more closely in line with what Kenneth Moler describes as the novel of the "Young Lady's Introduction to the World." This heroine is, according to a contemporary review, "just so accomplished and so

modest a young lady as we wished to find her." Unwillingly
exposed to London social life, the gentle Louisa is stalked by
rakes, loved by a proper hero, and after many adventures, finally rewarded with domestic bliss. Despite their differences
in general outline, however, these two novels each have
characteristics burlesqued in Austen's early work.

Northanger Abbey opens with the famous description of
Catherine the anti-heroine, in which we learn that, oddly
enough, both of her parents are still living. Neither Julia nor
Louisa, genuine sentimental heroines, are so favored. Julia's
mother died a few years after
the heroine's birth, and she
loses her father before the end
of the first volume of her tale.
Louisa is even more unfortunate, as she grieves for the
death of two fathers, discover-
ing from her mother's deathbed
confession that the man she
had previously mourned was
only legally her father. Her real
father was a Russian prince,
whom Louisa had in fact once
met by chance, but who died
shortly thereafter. Catherine,
possessed of two healthy, happy
parents, as well as nine broth-

Jane Austen

ers and sisters, does indeed fall short of familial standards
for heroines, who, like both Julia and Louisa, should also be
sans siblings.

As for youthful employments, we are told that Catherine
preferred boys' play to "the more heroic enjoyments of infancy, nursing a dormouse, [or] feeding a canary-bird." Elizabeth Hervey remains silent as to Louisa's animal-loving inclinations, but Julia more than makes up the deficiency. Her
favorite local cottage child is little Peggy, whom she once observed "taking some flies out of a bowl of water, and placing
them in the sun, where they shook their wet wings, and
were assisted in the operation of drying themselves by
Peggy; who put her face very close to the table, and endeav-
oured to revive them with her warm breath." Such kindness
is endearing to Julia, who had "frequently been engaged in
the very same business of rescuing flies from destruction;

and, when she saw a worm lying in her path, had often conveyed it to a place of safety among the untrodden grass." As for aiding birds, she is willing to pay for the privilege: "In her way, she saw a young bird that was unable to fly, hopping on the pavement. A boy seized it, whom she bribed with a shilling to relinquish his prize."

Another of Julia's accomplishments as a heroine is displayed when the ungrateful bird escapes from her. She mourns its loss with a painfully sentimental twenty-four line elegy, of which the following is typical:

> I would with lavish crumbs my Bird have fed,
> And bought a crystal cup to wet thy bill;
> I would have made of down and moss thy bed,
> Soft, though not fashion'd with a Thrush's skill.

Catherine falls considerably short in this area of expertise, as Julia's first poem was composed at age eight. But "though [Catherine] could not write sonnets, she brought herself to read them."

Music is an area in which Catherine is once again outdone by the heroines who precede her, since "there seemed no chance of her throwing a whole party into raptures by a prelude on the pianoforte, of her own composition." Louisa, however, is more than equal to this task:

> Louisa modestly took Miss Bensley's place at the harpsichord; and after a prelude, which occasioned the *connoisseurs* to cast upon each other very significant looks, she executed the piece with such taste and justness, as astonished the rest of the performers. The room echoed with *brava! brava!* every body was delighted with the composition. . . . Upon which she played a *rondeaux*, which enchanted them all; and every one was desirous of knowing who composed it—but nothing further could be learned, than that it was the composition of a friend; and by a faint blush that over-spread her cheek as she spoke, Mr. Melcomb suspected it was her own, which indeed was the case.

Of all such accomplishments requisite for heroines, we learn that Catherine's "greatest deficiency was in the pencil—she had no notion of drawing—not enough even to attempt a sketch of her lover's profile, that she might be detected in the design." On this point both she and Julia must concede to Louisa, "who had an exquisite sense of the beauties of nature, and could in a masterly style delineate them." She also finds a more solid means of reproducing a likeness of her absent lover, when she takes up modeling in wax and "plaister of Paris." Her attempted bust of Apollo takes on instead the form of her beloved Lord Danefield, as a visiting friend coyly points out to her—"Louisa, who had imagined this bust, placed high on a press, would have escaped observation, coloured extremely." Lord Danefield himself finally sees this flattering work at the novel's conclusion, generating by his pleasure pretty blushes from "the amiable artist."

Julia and Louisa both display many of the accomplishments that were standard for heroines of late eighteenth century novels. The novels in which they appear, however, also illustrate a number of more specific points addressed in *Northanger Abbey*. Austen attacks "that ungenerous and impolitic custom so common with novel writers, of degrading by their contemptuous censure the very performances, to the number of which they are themselves adding. . . . Alas! if the heroine of one novel be not patronized by the heroine of another, from whom can she expect protection and regard?" Both Julia and Louisa are guilty of sinning against their sister heroines. Julia's favorite poets are, like those of so many heroines, [Alexander] Pope and [James] Thomson, and at the home of her uncle, she enjoys the "best new publications . . . from town." But when asked if she has read the latest popular novel of sensibility, she replies, "No indeed I have not."

Louisa too rejects novels, although not so much by inclination as by training. Placed in the home of her grandmother at her legal father's dying request, this guardian's death prompts her grasping mother to demand Louisa's presence in London, where Lady Roseville attempts to entertain her daughter after her own fashion:

> Louisa perceived that most of the books in this collection, had been very much read; indeed so much so, that she cared not to touch them; however, taking down some of the cleanest, she found they were all novels. This was a species of reading unknown to her, as her grandmother had entirely discouraged it: but the want of books, and a page or two she had run over, in one of them, exciting her curiosity, tempted her to take it—when checking herself suddenly, "Why should I," thought she, "do *now*, what I would not have done some months since?"

Virtue triumphs, and is even rewarded, as she finally discovers "an odd volume or two of Shakespeare" with which to pass her time.

The character and function of Louisa's vain, foolish mother provides another parallel with Austen's parodic text, as she does much to "promote the general distress of the work." Deemed an unfit guardian by her father, Lady Roseville has been unacquainted with Louisa since the heroine's infancy. She proves an even more alarming candidate for the mock description of Mrs. Allen than does Fanny Burney's Madame Duval, as a person sure to make a heroine miserable, "whether by her imprudence, vulgarity, or jealousy—whether by intercepting her letters, ruining her character, or turning her out of doors." Lady Roseville introduces Louisa to a superficial and petty social circle, scheming to get her the wealthiest husband she can manage, and when Lord Pompouston seems the best bet, she shamelessly arranges private meetings between them, against Louisa's will.

Every heroine needs a champion for protection from rakes and unwanted suitors like Lord Pompouston, especially when such boors are encouraged by an unfit guardian. While Austen's Catherine experiences not one "lucky overturn to introduce [her] to the hero," Louisa is so favored, meeting Lord Danefield when her chairmen, "far from sober," overset her into the path of an oncoming carriage. When Louisa's growing love for her rescuer threatens her mother's schemes, his letters are intercepted by Lady Roseville. Finally deciding that boldness is best, her mother actually arranges to have Lord Pompouston carry Louisa off, in the familiar carriage abduction scene, mocked in miniature by Austen when John Thorpe drives the protesting Catherine away from Bath, making "odd noises" to his horse.

True to the theme of the "Young Lady's Introduction to the World," Louisa is much more in the public eye than is Julia. Her first major social appearance is greeted with pleasure:

> Louisa was confused at observing that she excited general attention: a momentary pause took place, as it were by common consent in conversation; a cessation of depredations on the cakes and muffins ensued; some cups were suspended from the lips; and at last a buz of admiration broke forth, and was quickly echoed through the room.

Catherine is contented with a humbler debut, since, of all those who see her, "not one . . . started with rapturous wonder on beholding her, no whisper of eager inquiry ran round the room, nor was she once called a divinity by any body." Julia's tale is less concerned with society, and more with her relationship to her friend Charlotte. One fine evening "these young ladies appeared at dinner dressed alike, and with the most graceful simplicity." That sincere friend, Isabella Thorpe, tries to prompt Catherine to a similar display: "But, my dearest Catherine, have you settled what to wear on your head tonight? I am determined at all events to be dressed exactly like you. The men take notice of *that* sometimes you know."

Julia and her friend share an outing of which Catherine would have been jealous, when they trek off to examine "the ruins of an old abbey." "Eager to explore every part of the ruins," Julia clambers about the "decayed" staircases and "shattered towers," finally reaching a proper spot for heroinely reflections:

> Julia gazed from the turret on the sublime landscape which surrounded her, and the venerable ruins, with that solemn emotion so grateful to a contemplative mind. "Surely," thought she, (in the fervor of an elevated spirit,) "surely the inhabitants of this retreat were happy!"

Catherine, who finds it "wonderful that her friends [Henry and Eleanor] should be so little elated by the possession of such a home" as Northanger Abbey, is disappointed in her hopes of exploring an abbey "just like what one reads about" when she visits the Tilney's modernized estate. The works of Ann Radcliffe, so frequently mentioned by Austen, are most commonly identified with Catherine's expectations, but sentimental fiction of the period prior to the appearance of Radcliffe's works often contained gothic elements—indeed some critics seem to have a "greater sensitivity" to distinctions between the gothic and the sentimental than probably existed at the time.

While emotional sentimental heroines could find beauty in gothic scenes, there were some shortcomings to an excess of sensibility, and these did not escape Austen's notice. Despite all of her divine qualities, Mrs. Hervey's Louisa does have one large fault—jealousy. Several incidents bring forth this trait, until she is finally reprimanded by a close friend. When Louisa sees Lord Danefield escorting a pretty young woman into a coach on one of the less reputable streets in London, she immediately assumes the worst, suffering "a sensation entirely new," although soon to be felt again. The woman proves to be his half-sister. Austen's Catherine conducts herself much more gracefully in a similar situation, when she sees Henry

> talking with interest to a fashionable and pleasing-looking young woman, who leant on his arm, and whom Catherine

immediately guessed to be his sister; thus unthinkingly throwing away a fair opportunity of considering him lost to her for ever. . . . Therefore, instead of turning of a deathlike paleness, and falling in a fit on Mrs. Allen's bosom, Catherine sat erect, in the perfect use of her senses.

Catherine's pragmatic behavior, viewed with an eye to Louisa's sensibility, is less a product of "instinctive good sense" than a means by which Austen targets sentimental authors as well as gothic, perhaps with specific reference to Elizabeth Hervey's jealous Louisa.

DEVELOPING A GREATER UNDERSTANDING OF *NORTHANGER ABBEY*

No single parallel here examined is so striking as to be absolutely conclusive, but their cumulative effect is to suggest that *Julia* and *Louisa* were works familiar to Jane Austen, even if only as two of many Julias and Louisas intended by Henry's remark. Neither Elizabeth Hervey nor Helen Maria Williams were obscure authors in Austen's youth. The former, born Elizabeth March (sometimes spelled Marsh), was half-sister to William Beckford, the author of *Vathek*. While her works appeared anonymously, *Louisa*, her second novel, was the subject of at least six reviews upon its publication. Williams, "one of the earliest, and most ardent, English Jacobins," [according to Gina Luria] was a controversial writer associated with Mary Wollstonecraft and other radicals, and her novel *Julia* generated no fewer than 13 contemporary reviews.

Knowledge of these novels provides a more complete context for Austen's works. A modern reader acquainted with the novels of Ann Radcliffe, Charlotte Smith, and Fanny Burney has a glimpse of Austen's literary background, but although they may be the best of her contemporaries, they were only three of the many writers producing popular fiction. The seven "horrid" novels provide a richer context for the gothic elements of Austen's burlesque, but one must remember that *Northanger Abbey*, a title so evocative of the gothic, was not necessarily Austen's choice for this posthumous publication. She had originally intended *Susan*, and then *Catherine*, titles that clearly tie her work to the sentimental genre. While such novels as *Julia* and *Louisa* may have a limited appeal today, this does not diminish the impact they may have had on their contemporary readers.

The implications of a closer look at Austen's neglected contemporaries, however, extend beyond establishing a fuller context for her works. Previous readings of *Northanger Abbey* have focused predominantly on its gothic elements. But the more connections that can be drawn to the sentimental genre, the more one must admit that readings to date have been somewhat lopsided. The principal criticism aimed at *Northanger Abbey* is that the Bath and Northanger sections are ill-balanced; a greater knowledge of the extent to which Austen burlesques the sentimental novel as well as the gothic can help to bring our vision of the work back into equilibrium. Thus, in addition to the pleasure one can gain by rediscovering lively and interesting works long fallen out of favor, the modern reader and critic can in fact benefit from joining Henry Tilney in "a knowledge of Julias and Louisas."

The Influences of Roman Satire in Byron's *Don Juan*

Frederick L. Beaty

Frederick L. Beaty explains how the works of Roman satirists Horace, Juvenal, and Persius heavily shaped the form of Lord Byron's satirical poem *Don Juan*. For example, in Canto V, Byron imitates the form of Roman satire by having Don Juan and Johnson discuss Stoicism; similar dialogues are found in the writings of Persius and Horace. Juvenal influenced Byron's depiction of Don Juan's sexual encounters, in particular Juan's dalliance with Gulbeyaz; additionally, Juvenal's use of invective and the role played by fate in his satires are reflected in *Don Juan*. Beaty concludes that it was most likely Juvenal's writing that deepened Byron's understanding of satire. Beaty is a professor emeritus of English at Indiana University in Bloomington and the author of *Light from Heaven: Love in British Romantic Literature, The Ironic World of Evelyn Waugh: A Study of Eight Novels,* and *Byron the Satirist,* the book from which the following article has been excerpted.

The form of *Don Juan* is so indeterminate as virtually to defy categorization. Since the classical epic, Roman satire, Italian epic romance, mock-heroic poetry, the picaresque novel, Restoration comedy, the realistic novel, the novel of manners, the pantomime, Gothic romance, the ballad, the lyric, and neoclassical satire have all left their imprint on the poem, it is not surprising that the receptacle containing such varied ingredients should be amorphous. Critics who have felt uneasy about calling *Don Juan* a "hold-all" have resorted to designating it as a metrical novel, a mock-epic, an epic

Excerpted from *Byron the Satirist* by Frederick L. Beaty (DeKalb: Northern Illinois University Press, 1985). Copyright © 1985 by Northern Illinois University Press. Reprinted with permission.

carnival, an epic of negation, epic satire, or merely satire. While excellent cases can be made for all these labels, none is utterly satisfactory for the poem as a whole. One of the few delineations with which no critics would cavil is James R. Thompson's description of *Don Juan* as "a kind of generic explosion produced by the nineteenth-century pressure to redefine form in highly personal terms."

A POEM WITH NO REAL FORM

What is undeniable, in any case, is that the form, or formlessness, accurately reflects Byron's view of life and man's disordered, incongruous, and unpredictable world. His concept of artistic form, as [Jerome J.] McGann has maintained, is not concerned with internal unity but, in the Horatian [referring to the Roman satirist Horace] tradition, with rhetoric and function. Form, either in the classical sense of a preconceived mold or in the Romantic sense of a product of organic development, has little meaning for *Don Juan*. So long as a poetical work was "simple and entire," as Byron translated the Horatian dictum in *Hints from Horace*, and also was organized in such a way as to express most effectively what the poet had to say, form could take care of itself. Byron's repeated assertions that the cantos of *Don Juan*, whether organized around topics or episodic narrative, could go on almost indefinitely suggest a looseness of structure and an open-endedness that challenge conventional notions of form. The shapelessness of *Don Juan*, however, was not a serious problem with regard to satire. Since its Roman inception, satire has been thought of as a hodgepodge (*farrago*), a medley, or a miscellaneous collection. It has tended to be so unstructured that, as Northrop Frye affirmed, "a kind of parody of form seems to run all through its tradition." Acquaintance with the tradition, which included many varieties of satire and different levels of style appropriate to them, had taught Byron that there was actually no prescribed form.

He was sufficiently skilled as a classicist to appreciate what the Romans called formal satire. In Latin *satura* designated only a particular literary genre—a seemingly unordered poem mixing unfavorable criticism with moral observations. In English, however, the term *satire* could be applied to any artistic composition in which the author's inception was to arouse contempt for his subject. More loosely, it might refer to isolated passages in compositions that were not predominantly derogatory, to the temper characterizing such works, or even to the techniques employed to degrade. It is revealing that in letters and conversations Byron most frequently referred to *Don Juan* as a satire. It is also significant that early reviewers saw the poem primarily as satire—on everything, including the epic. And whatever the generic modulations of the poem, its substance is undeniably permeated by the satiric spirit, even in instances when that spirit, as both Ernest J. Lovell and Alvin B. Kernan have observed, is so thoroughly blended with either comedy or tragedy that it can hardly be identified as "serious" satire. Since there was no satiric form adequate to a large composition, a more comprehensive genre, such as the epic, was needed as a carrier—one in which a variety of intentions, including the satiric, could function. Within this matrix Byron was able to incorporate not only many kinds of satire but in one instance, the Constantinople episode, an illustration of *satura.*

THE USE OF ROMAN SATIRE IN CANTO V

His conscious adaptation of both the form and substance of Roman satire in Canto V suggests that he wished that portion to be seen in the light of a continuing tradition. This imitation was his way of announcing his genre and establishing his pedigree. His two introductory stanzas beginning that canto advertise his intention of forsaking "amorous writing" in favor of an edifying variety that attaches morals to every error and attacks all the passions. Properly interpreted, the narrator's role becomes that of the Roman satirist with Stoic[1] inclinations. Moreover, the dialogue in which Johnson explains his Stoic philosophy to Juan (V.13–25) is an authentic replica of the dialogue form in which both Horace and [Roman poet and philosopher] Persius treated Stoic doctrines. Horace actually invented the satiric dialogue and used it with subtle irony to involve prolocutor and adversary in a dramatic skit. Persius, though strongly inclined toward dramatic conversations even when the presence of his opponent in a debate had to be imagined, used the Horatian innovation as framework for only two whole satires, while Juvenal was even less disposed toward dialogue form. It was

1. Stoicism is a Greek philosophy that believes that in order to be wise, man must accept the rule of natural law and live free from passion, joy, grief, and other strong feelings.

[Alexander] Pope, in his *Imitations of Horace,* who proved to be most skillful of all in pitting speakers against one another in an evolving discussion. Pope's example probably inspired Byron to attempt a similar feat.

The Stoic "paradox" enunciated by Johnson—that all those who have failed to liberate themselves from their passions are enslaved—was part of the Roman satiric tradition, having been used by Horace and Persius in dialogue form. In Horace's Satire 11.3 Damasippus expounds the topos that all who are not wise enough to be masters of themselves are mad and thereupon accuses Horace, cast in this case as the adversary, of madness. Similarly in Satire 11.7 Horace's slave Davus, in the role of prolocutor, tries to convince his "enslaved" master that only Stoic philosophers who have renounced all passions (men like Davus himself, of course) are free. Drawing on both of the foregoing Stoic dialogues of Horace, Persius's fifth satire employs toward its conclusion an imagined conversation between the satirist and a hypothetical freed slave to demonstrate that only philosophers are free.

In view of the popularity of Stoic discourses, Johnson's comments on universal slavery in Canto V of *Don Juan* might not be linked specifically to Persius's fifth satire were it not for Byron's unmistakable verbal borrowing from notes offered by [Martin] Madan to his translation of Juvenal and Persius. Drawing on Madan's explanation of Persius's farfetched metaphors, which are presumably based on the shedding of snakeskin, the fluttering of limed birds, and the struggling of beasts in nets, Byron clustered all three images in the following passage:

> some grand mistake
> Casts off its bright skin yearly like the snake.
>
> 'Tis true, it gets another bright and fresh,
>   Or fresher, brighter; but the year gone through,
> This skin must go the way too of all flesh,
>   Or sometimes only wear a week or two;—
> Love's the first net which spreads its deadly mesh;
>   Ambition, Avarice, Vengeance, Glory, glue
> The glittering lime-twigs of our latter days,
> Where still we flutter on for pence or praise. (V.21.7–22.8)

Three of man's ensnaring passions in life's progressive disillusionment—love, ambition, and avarice—are among the six deterrents to liberty discussed in Persius's fifth; and in Horace's two Stoic dialogues they are also attacked as prime obstacles to equanimity. Vengeance and glory, on the other hand, are strongly identified with Juvenal, particularly in Satire X, Byron's favorite.

BYRON'S TREATMENT OF STOICISM

Byron also had precedents in Roman satire for his ironic presentation of Stoicism from several perspectives. Persius, who would have his readers believe that he never wavers from adherence to Stoic tenets, concedes at the close of his fifth satire that his philosophy is not for ignoramuses like the coarse centurion. Horace, in his two Stoic dialogues, presents the advocates of Stoicism as unreliable counselors— Damasippus, a social outcast as well as former madman, and Davus, an insolent slave; both fail to convert the satirist, whom they accuse of being enslaved by follies. But whereas Horace merely implies that the rigorous demands of Stoicism are more readily postulated than practiced, Byron's narrator makes that inference explicit: Juan's recent misfortunes are said to have been enough "to shake a stoic" (V.9.1), and later when Juan ceases weeping he is said to have "called back the stoic to his eyes" (V.121.5).

Yet Johnson, despite outward manifestations of English sangfroid, does not qualify as a true Stoic. Indeed his reliance on fate or *fortuna* as the ruling force in men's lives recalls Juvenal's association of fatalism with false Stoics who do not live by what they preach (Satires II.65; IX.32,35). Even while claiming to be inured to life through crushing adversities, Johnson is sufficiently proved to offer consolation to the tender-hearted Juan. What the former advocates is not so much true Stoicism as an attitude of resignation. Declaring that knowledge can be gained through viewing one's present state from the proper perspective, he argues that the experience of slavery will teach a man how better to behave when a master (V23.5–8). His ironic undercutting of Stoicism, when he asserts that its requisite detachment from life is purchased at the exorbitant price of human feelings, has parallels in Horace, who concludes his Stoic dialogues with contrived jests or congés that question man's ability to abide by Stoic principles.

Byron's skill in combining various ingredients drawn from Roman satire into a traditional satiric form deserves special attention. Though the subject of Johnson's discourse derives primarily from Persius, the general tone of the dialogue more closely resembles the Horatian mixture of genial humor and wry cynicism than the earnest didacticism of Persius. Yet it was Byron's originality in readapting classical materials that earned him a place as a contributor to the tradition. His conversion of metaphorical enslavement into physical reality and

his use of Constantinople's slave market as a microcosm of mercantile society, where everyone offers himself to the highest bidder, ingeniously and vastly enriched the possibilities for a thematic conflict between freedom and slavery in that episode. Even Stoic philosophy is so modernized as to be assimilable into Robert Walpole's truism on human venality ("all have prices, / . . . according to their vices"— V.27.7–8) and to be assailable ultimately as a philosophy of insensibility ("To feel for none is

Lord Byron

the true social art / Of the world's stoics—men without a heart"—V.25.7–8). And the dialogue between Johnson and Juan is more than an unresolved debate on Stoicism. As a dramatic mode of dialectic, it stimulates each speaker to a revelation of his own perspective, as well as to a deeper perception of the limitations inherent in his own outlook. Through his naive questioning of Johnson's cynical approach, Juan serves as friendly adversary or *provocateur* in evoking the differences between sentimental youth and disillusioned age. One of Byron's finest achievements in this *sermo* is the unexpected combination of a crescendo suggesting a modified Stoicism as the key to survival and an ironic coda questioning its validity as a guide to life.

Possibly because Byron saw a number of parallels between Constantinople, which he called "Rome transplanted" (V.86.8), and Rome under the early caesars, he drew many other suggestions for his fifth canto from Roman satire and thereby emphasized further his connection with that still vital tradition. The narrator's frequent references to the role of capricious fortune in that section are reminiscent of Juvenal and, to a lesser degree, Horace rather than of Moslem belief. It is likely that Byron had mentally assimilated the extensive commentary Madan wrote for Juvenal's tenth satire on the significance of Fortuna in pagan Rome. Certainly Byron was indebted to the substance of two Juvenalian satires (VI and X) for the encounter involving Juan and the lustful sultana Gulbeyaz. For ideas, phraseology, and analogies he also drew on Madan's notes about the nymphomaniac empress Messalina and her determination to force the handsome Gaius Silius to become her husband. Much of the broad sexual jesting in the fifth canto echoes that of Juvenal. Castration, for example, in addition to being an accepted Turkish practice, may have been suggested by hints in Juvenal's tenth that Madan had explicated. While circumcision remained a notable difference between Christian and Moslem in Byron's day, as his earlier letters observed, he would also have recalled the recurrent jests in Horace, Persius, and Juvenal about Jewish circumcision. Juan's transvestism, as well as its sexual overtones, had precedents in Juvenal and in Madan's notes to Satires II and X. But throughout that episode it is not so much the imitation of the model that deserves study as the ingenious transformation of Juvenalian materials in the alembic of Byron's imagination. Byron's achievement, in altering even the "tragic satire" of Juvenal into half-serious comedy dealing with feminine lust, masculine chastity, marital fidelity, and tyranny over all that should be free, shows how completely he could absorb the ingredients of Roman satire into his own creation.

DON JUAN AS A NEW KIND OF EPIC

While the imitation of *satura* is evident only in Canto V, the overall randomness of *Don Juan* suggests satiric content. It is primarily through the satiric spirit, especially as it is assimilated into epic form, that Byron's satire functions. Despite the poem's open defiance of epic conventions, the narrator repeatedly claims that *Don Juan* is an epic and that its contents (love, war, shipwreck, and even a "view of hell") qualify it for that designation. There is good reason, furthermore, to believe that Byron took those claims seriously, that he intended something more than another comic epic in the Italian tradition. It would be easy, especially in the early cantos, to assert that *Don Juan* is a mock-epic since that subgenre not only incorporates satire in its burlesque of epic conventions but also uses the ideals of previous epics to illustrate, by allusion, the contrast between earlier greatness and contemporary pettiness. But as Brian Wilkie has shown, *Don Juan* is not just a mock-epic. Byron was determined that, unlike his "epic brethren gone before," he would write a *true* epic depicting man and his world realistically. On the assumption that *Don Juan* in scope and purpose deserved to be compared to Homer's *Iliad,* Byron told Thomas Medwin in late 1821 or early 1822 that his poem was "an epic as much in the spirit of our day as the Iliad was in Homer's." Evidently he thought it mirrored the religious, political, and social attitudes of his own era as comprehensively and accurately as Homer's epic had reflected his age. Byron's invocation of Homer's aid before the siege of Ismail (VII, 79–80), his use of language less formal and stylized than Virgil's or [John] Milton's, and his rejection of a providential or teleological design for background of the protagonist's "heroism" indicate that Byron in some ways felt a closer affinity with Homer than with the later epic poets. But fundamental changes in the inherited tradition were necessary to produce a modern epic depicting the ideals—or lack of them—in contemporary society, and satire was essential in sharpening its negative features.

When in 1823 Byron called *Don Juan* an "Epic Satire" (XIV.99.6), he acknowledged its hybrid nature. His poetic commentary on [Miguel de Cervante's novel] *Don Quixote* (XIII.8–11)—upon which [George M.] Ridenour has elaborated—suggests the relationship that Byron apparently saw between satire and epic. Even though Cervantes may have assumed that in our corrupt world only a fool or a madman could champion chivalric values, he was not, in Byron's judgment, ridiculing the noble idealism for which Quixote fights. Cervantes' "hero" is "right" in

> Redressing injury, revenging wrong,
> > To aid the damsel and destroy the caitiff;
> Opposing singly the united strong,
> > From foreign yoke to free the helpless native.
> (XIII.10.1–4)

Yet we smile at the spectacle the deluded knight makes of himself, and, reflection on the folly of defending virtue, we realize the melancholy plight in which Cervantes has involved us. Thus what Cervantes may have begun as satire on the absurdities of knight-errantry resulted in a "real Epic unto all who have thought" (XIII.9.8). By demolishing the traditional concept of heroism, he destroyed the old form of epic romance. In its place he provided a genuine, realistic epic, the only kind viable in a skeptical, disillusioned age.

This reading of *Don Quixote* has implications for Byron's interpretation of epic satire in *Don Juan*. Like Cervantes, Byron strove through satire to banish a false vision of life. In the course of achieving that goal he produced, like Cervantes, a literary form that radically readapted epic traditions, the epic hero, and the very idea of heroism—a form that could integrate other literary genres into itself and accommodate satire as part of its realistic approach. The union of such an epic and satire was more compatible than might have at first appeared, for the traditions of the two genres already met on common ground. Love, war, shipwreck, banquets, and glimpses of Hades, essential ingredients in the epic, were also standard fare in Roman *satura* and neoclassical adaptations. In *Don Juan* epic of a negative thrust could easily exist in symbiotic relationship with satire. The epic element, impelled by narrative, was identifiable with the onward momentum of life; the satiric, conversely, with whatever threatened man's progress. True heroism and idealism, however rare, were not to be scorned, though their goals were usually unattainable and their adherents often appeared foolish to a cynical world. This ironic situation, as Byron saw it, represented the dilemma of modern man, and "Epic Satire" was his way of embodying it.

Quite likely the term *epic satire* also had another association for Byron. Although he may have thought of *Don Juan* in its earliest stages as primarily in the *genus tenue* and the casual Horatian mode, as the poem developed more grandiose proportions he acquired a loftier sense of its mission—one comparable to the Juvenalian concept of satire in the *genus grande*. Particularly from careful study of Juvenal's Satires I, VI, X, and XV, Byron learned that true-to-life satire might be as edifying as tragedy or epic. Even though Juvenal respected the great epics of the past, he had the utmost contempt for poetasters of his day who strained beyond their abilities to attempt the highest genres. Traditional epic and tragedy, with their artificial conventions, impracticable ideals, and hackneyed mythological subjects, seemed no longer viable to Juvenal because they were irrelevant to contemporary life. What was needed, in view of the corruption permeating every stratum of Roman society, was a literature of truth rather than of literary invention—in short, one that depicted reality as Juvenal saw it. If satire was to supersede the outworn genres in the old poetic hierarchy and assume their instructive functions, the satirist was obliged to aspire to a *genus grande* that would approximate, even while radically readapting, epic form. In practice Juvenal substantiated those assumptions through elevated rhetoric, an impassioned style, and a heroic determination to amend society through exposure of wrongdoing. A mock invocation to Calliope in his fourth satire (ll.34–36) suggests that a satirist who records the truth has transcended the need of epic inspiration, and he dismisses her as peremptorily as Byron would later with "Hail, Muse! *et cetera*" (*DJ* III.1.1). Juvenal's frequent imitation of epic, whether with serious intent or, when style was inappropriate to subject matter, for humorous effect, further showed that he strove for a nobler goal than that ordinarily associated with the satires of Horace and Persius. It may well be that Juvenal's works, to which Byron repeatedly returned over the years, deepened his concept of satire so that it evolved beyond a youthful lashing out at whatever displeased him into a sophisticated view of life encompassing all things human.

Mark Twain as One of America's Great Satirists

Ernest Jackson Hall

Ernest Jackson Hall contends that Mark Twain was
one of America's greatest satirists. Hall explains that
the basis of Twain's satire was the exposing of false-
hood and sentimentality. For example, in *A Connecticut Yankee in King Arthur's Court,* Twain targets sentimental nostalgia for chivalry and other obsolete
notions. Another of Twain's works, *The Innocents
Abroad,* exposes the false sentimentality and reactions of American tourists in Europe. Twain also
mocked political and religious hypocrisies. Hall was
the author of *The Satirical Element in the American
Novel,* the source of the following selection.

Samuel Langhorne Clemens, "Mark Twain," (1835–1910) is,
after [James Fenimore] Cooper, our most extensive satirist.
In quality his satire far surpasses that of the earlier writer.
Much of Cooper's satire grew out of attempts to vent personal spite upon his critics or others whom he considered
his enemies. The result is that a great deal of his satire is
narrow, ill-considered, and lacking in interest unless one
studies it in connection with the particular episode in the
author's life which called it forth. The satire of Mark Twain,
on the other hand, comes from an inborn hatred of all sham,
hypocrisy, and sentimentality, wherever and however manifested. Getting his early training in the rough and matter-of-
fact life of the fast-growing West, where a man had to stand
or fall largely by virtue of his own intrinsic merits, this hatred of the "gilded" was intensified and deepened till it became one of the dominant qualities of his character, and so
of his writings. On the river-boats, in the mining camps, at

the editorial desk of the small newspaper, he lived in an atmosphere of rough humor, practical jokes, and irreverent comment. The air was full of incongruities and exaggerations. It is not strange, therefore, that the earlier writings, particularly, of Mark Twain are full of burlesque and boisterous laughter. The only trouble is that he often showed too much of the Philistine spirit. From mawkish sentimentality he sometimes went to the opposite extreme where nothing was sacred and where conventions were merely clods to be kicked into the ditch. Fortunately, however, this was not always the case, for at heart he was entirely sincere, and, if he occasionally overstepped the bounds of good taste, the effect of his fracture of the rules was at least to call attention very forcibly to the narrowness and senselessness of much that had previously been accepted as the only becoming mode.

Much that Mark Twain wrote cannot properly be classed as fiction, though there is in nearly everything that he produced a fictional element. Primarily a humorist and satirist, he lacked the studied technique and painstaking patience necessary for the development of a great plot or a great character. His ability lay rather in the depiction of a single episode. The result is that even such of his works as may be called novels are episodic and lacking in constructive finish.

EXAMPLES OF TWAIN'S SATIRE

Beginning with "The Innocents Abroad" (1869), his works which contain any considerable amount of satire are "Roughing It" (1872), "The Gilded Age" (1873), "The Adventures of Tom Sawyer" (1876), "The Prince and the Pauper" (1882), "A Connecticut Yankee in King Arthur's Court" (1889), "The American Claimant" (1892), "The Man That Corrupted Hadleyburg" (1899), and "Captain Stormfield's Visit to Heaven" (1908). As stated in the previous paragraph, opinions differ widely as to the right which each of these has to be classed as fiction. However, there is in all of them a fictional element, which would seem to entitle them to a place in the present discussion.

Mark Twain's first great success was his "The Innocents Abroad," an account of his visit to the Mediterranean and adjoining countries. On the surface it was merely a funny man's story of a trip and was so considered by a great many readers and then laid aside. Underneath the fun, however, is the serious purpose to expose the sham sentimentality, sham appreciation of the great and the beautiful, and sham reference for things of the Old World which had so often characterized the traveler in foreign lands. Though it is true, as previously stated, that he occasionally errs in the opposite direction, and seems sometimes to forfeit our respect, nevertheless his pages contain more real truth than did most of the travel-books of the time, and their effect upon later books of the sort has been of a decidedly salutary nature.

"Roughing It" contains less of the satirical than does the earlier book. Purporting to be an autobiographical sketch of a trip through the West, it boastfully proclaims the superior qualities of this region, at the same time laughing rather boisterously at the older and less favored sections of the world.

In "The Gilded Age" (with Charles Dudley Warner) and "The American Claimant" the satire is chiefly of the corrupt political conditions which characterized city, state, and nation during the latter half of the nineteenth century. Colonel Sellers is the central character in both; around him is woven a great deal of noisy burlesque, coupled with stinging thrusts at those who made of public office little else than an easy means to private gain.

Of his next, and best known novel, "The Adventures of Tom Sawyer," little need be said here. It contains the least satire of all his works under consideration. The satire, where it does occur, is purely incidental and is no outstanding quality as in the other cases.

MOCKING THE COURTLY LIFE

Hatred of sham and sentimentality and hatred of monarchial despotism find expression in "The Prince and the Pauper" and "A Connecticut Yankee in King Arthur's Court." Though not dealing with native material, except in so far as the Yankee reveals American characteristics, both books are nevertheless American in tone, since the contrast is always between democracy and monarchy, between reality and superstition. "The Prince and the Pauper" is partly a children's story of how Prince Edward and Tom Canty, a beggar boy, exchange clothes and positions, and partly a grown-ups' satire upon kings and courts and courtly artificialities. Much more scathing in its satirical lashings is the "Connecticut Yankee." As "The Innocents Abroad" voiced a reaction against the sentimentality connected with material relics of the Old World, so this book voices a reaction against the sentimentality connected with the so-called chivalry of the Middle Ages. It is throughout a rather untrammeled burlesque of such writings as Malory's "Morte d'Arthur" and Tennyson's "Idylls of the King." It is true that Mark Twain ascribes to King Arthur's day many faults which did not exist then but which were characteristic of the author's own or intervening centuries; yet, in the main, he paints a very realistic picture of the sordidness and oppression and misery which fed the flower of knighthood, and which had been largely forgotten or glossed over by other writers.

In "The Man That Corrupted Hadleyburg" he satirizes the folly of greed and the hypocritical smugness of those who pray not to be led into temptation and then weakly succumb to the first real temptation which comes to them. Again, in "Captain Stormfield's Visit to Heaven" he satirized the, to him, absurd picture of heaven as given to us by the Hebrews. That he could not altogether free himself from the conventional belief in a city of golden streets seems to be evidenced by the fact that this latter story was kept in manuscript for more than half of its author's lifetime and published only two years before his death.

And now what shall we say of Mark Twain's position as a satirist among American writers of fiction? If it be granted that the writings discussed in the preceding paragraphs are fiction, and in the broader sense of imagination playing upon and transforming facts, they are fiction, then their author is entitled to a position near, if not at, the top. Many others have written greater novels and short stories, many others have combined satire more artistically with fiction, but none has used satire more extensively, more sincerely, or, on the whole, more effectively than he.

CHAPTER 3

Modern Satire

 Satire

Sinclair Lewis's Satires of Middle America

C. Hugh Holman

In the following essay, C. Hugh Holman shows how Sinclair Lewis wrote novels that satirized and mocked the experiences of small-town Midwesterners. Lewis's satire was filled with invective and caricature of people such as evangelical preachers, businessmen, and small-town matrons. In his guise as narrator, Lewis displays a superiority to almost all his characters and reveals their foibles and ridiculous aspirations. Holman, who died in 1981, was a professor of English at the University of North Carolina at Chapel Hill. He was a recipient of a Simon Guggenheim Fellowship and the author or editor of twenty-six books, including *The Roots of Southern Writing* and *Windows on the World: Essays on American Social Fiction.*

Sinclair Lewis, America's first Nobel laureate in literature, was the summation and epitome of the satiric and comic reaction to what he labeled the "Village Virus." Indeed, the Nobel citation read: "The 1930 Nobel Prize in Literature is awarded to Sinclair Lewis for his powerful and vivid art of description and his ability to use wit and humor in the creation of original characters." A native of Sauk Centre, Minnesota, Lewis was educated at Oberlin College and Yale University. In the 1920's he turned his attention back to the country of his childhood and adolescence and produced five novels that, despite a number of obvious weaknesses, seem to have a secure place in our national literature. These novels are *Main Street,* a satiric portrait of a small town huddled on the Great Plains; *Babbitt,* a portrait of a representative businessman in a typical small city in the Middle West; *Arrowsmith,* a portrait of the scientist as saint, of a physician pursuing truth with unselfish and absolute commitment, and an attack on the society that tries to inhibit and pervert his search; *Elmer Gantry*, a savagely comic portrait of a dishonest and insincere minister and of the world in which he works; and *Dodsworth*, a mellower satire, this time of Americans seeking culture in Europe. He was to produce ten more novels before his death in 1951, but none of them had the energy, vitality, and originality of the five that established his fame and, in fact, said just about all that he had to say of a world that he both loved and mocked for its painful inadequacies. Yet most of the novels published after *Dodsworth* remained grounded in the life of the Middle West, were couched in the language of the earlier works, and maintained many of the same attitudes, although mellowed by time, of his earlier years.

LEWIS'S NARRATIVE QUALITIES

Lewis was originally taken as a realist, partly because his great power of mimicry gave an apparent authenticity to the speech of his characters and partly because the massive research which he did in getting the surface details of the daily lives of his people precisely right cast an air of great accuracy over the world he represented. But Sinclair Lewis was really a satirist and a humorist, and in his use of the devices and methods of the satirist and humorist lie both his greatest strengths and his chief weaknesses.

As a humorist he belongs clearly in the tradition of Yankee humor, that of the shrewd and knowing peddler or the crackerbox philosopher. For the most important person in Lewis's best work is Lewis himself. It is he who sees with great clarity, describes with deflating directness, mocks, sneers at, condemns. Everywhere in his novels—and particularly in *Main Street* and *Babbitt*—the reader is listening to the narrator-novelist and indeed is being invited to share with him his sense of the incongruity and falseness of the world being described. Thus the novels become extended comic and satiric essays, with narrative exempla to illustrate and underscore the points. The most common posture of the narrator is that of detached observer and sardonic critic. The characters are seen from the outside, their words checked against their deeds, their actions presented mockingly. When we enter their thoughts, it is seldom to explore them as fully realized characters but rather to pinpoint a motive or make ridiculous an aspiration or dream. For example, when Carol Kennicott, in *Main Street,* is putting out plants in a park near the railroad station, Lewis says: "Passengers looking from trains saw her as a village woman of fading prettiness, incorruptible virtue, and no abnormalities . . . and all the while she saw herself running garlanded through the streets of Babylon." Certainly the interior glimpse is not intended to make an exploration of psychological depths but to deflate and to mock. The original plan of *Babbitt* was that it should represent a typical day in the life of a typical businessman. That plan still survives in the first seven chapters, one-fourth of the total book, and it is only after this eventless and typical day that the casual plot of Babbitt's futile efforts at rebellion get under way. Lewis's statement about Elmer Gantry is not unusual: "He had been sitting with a Bible and an evening paper in his lap, reading one of them." Nor is the description of Gantry praying in the pulpit of his church: "He turned to include the choir, and for the first time he saw that there was a new singer, a girl with charming ankles and lively eyes, with whom he would certainly have to become well acquainted. But the thought was so swift that it did not interrupt the paean of his prayer." No, Lewis is not drawing extended psychographs of people; he is exhibiting specimens as though they were insects in a display case, and when he penetrates their skin it is primarily to make them squirm.

This narrator is superior to his subjects. In the five big novels he presents only two characters who are treated with full sympathy, Martin Arrowsmith and Sam Dodsworth, and one, Carol Kennicott of *Main Street,* whom he likes but frequently mocks. The superiority he feels toward his people is based on his greater knowledge and his distance from them but, most important of all, it is based on his moral sense. To find the standard against which to measure these people in establishing this judgment of their morality, Lewis looks toward the past. He finds it in the sturdy pioneers, whom he often celebrates. *Main Street* begins: "On a hill by the Mississippi where Chippewas camped two generations ago. . . ." And it goes on to say, "The days of pioneering, of lassies in sunbonnets, and bears killed with axes in piney clearings, are deader now than Camelot; and a rebellious girl is the spirit of that bewildered empire called the American Middlewest." *Arrowsmith* opens with the protagonist's great-grandmother, as a girl of fourteen, driving a wagon in the

Ohio wilderness in the face of great adversity. It is what the towns and cities, the practices of business and the conventions of so-called polite society do to these pioneer virtues that Lewis is attacking, and it is the individualism and rugged independence which the pioneers exemplify to him whose passing he laments. It is little wonder that that most antisocial of American individualists, Henry David Thoreau, should have been one of his ideals.

This narrator is brash and even outrageous in his style. He flings at his satiric target not merely the customary satiric methods, but he brightens and sharpens his writing with vigorous metaphors. In *Elmer Gantry* he describes the workers in the "Charity Organization Society" as being "as

---

THE VARYING MOODS OF LEWIS'S SATIRE

Literary scholar Daniel R. Brown explains how the targets and quality of Sinclair Lewis's satire varied from novel to novel.

The over-all pattern of [Sinclair Lewis's] fiction is made more complex by the fact that he was not always certain of the things he disliked. Part of the paradox in his work is due to a steady, discernible ambivalence in his attitude toward many of the ideas and characters that he satirized. He always despised certain kinds of thinking and actions, cruelty and coarseness of speech, for example, but his attitude varied from novel to novel. If someone read only *Babbitt*, for example, he would not experience the breadth of Lewis's hatreds. For *Babbitt* is only one of Lewis's moods. If the reader catches him in another one, say in *Dodsworth* or *The Prodigal Parents*, it is very likely that he will see how much Lewis admired the "steadiness" and basic good sense of the upper-middle-class businessman. Furthermore, in one book Lewis praises liberalism; in another he makes fun of it. He ridicules Babbitt for lacking a sense of beauty; he smiles benignly on Doremus Jessup or Arrowsmith for the same weakness. Sometimes he ridicules the Communists with scorn, and at other times he singles them out for commendation.

His satire is at its best, its most exciting, when he is totally armed as an opponent, as he is in *It Can't Happen Here* and *Elmer Gantry*. In these novels, he is undoubtedly one-sided and unfair, but all satire is this way. When the attitude becomes inconsistent, it becomes watery and tepid.

Daniel R. Brown, "Lewis's Satire—A Negative Emphasis," *Renascence*, Winter 1966.

efficient and as tender as vermin-exterminators," and he says of a saloon that "it had the delicacy of a mining camp minus its vigor." In *Main Street* he says that the people at a party "sat up with gaiety as with a corpse." He declares of Terwillinger College, "You would not be likely to mistake Terwillinger College for an Old Folks' Home, because on the campus is a large rock painted with class numerals." Sometimes he writes scenes that are clearly boisterous comedy, such as this one about Elmer Gantry: "Elmer's eloquence increased like an August pumpkin. He went into the woods to practise. Once a small boy came up behind him, standing on a stump in a clearing, and upon being greeted with 'I denounce the abominations of your lascivious and voluptuous, uh, abominations,' he fled yelping, and never again was the same care-free youth."

THE TARGETS OF LEWIS'S SATIRE

Lewis is a satirist above all other things. While satire is often comic, its object is not to evoke mere laughter but laughter for a corrective purpose. It always has a target, an object which it attacks, such as pretense, falsity, deception, arrogance; and this target is held up to ridicule by the satirist's unmasking it. The satirist's vision is ultimately that of the cold-eyed realist, who penetrates shams and pretenses to reveal the truth. The simplest kind of satire is invective—that is, forthright and abusive language directed against a target so that it makes a sudden revelation of a damaging truth. Another kind of direct satire is exaggeration, by which the good characteristics are reduced and the evil or ridiculous ones are increased. Indirect satire whereby characters render themselves ridiculous by their actions and their speech is more subtle. Lewis as a satirist is usually direct and blunt. His favorite devices are invective and caricature, and in his role of unabashed and self-conscious narrator he can apply these methods directly.

His invective can be devastating. He wrote of small-town ladies as "creamy-skinned fair women, smeared with grease and chalk, gorgeous in the skins of beasts and the bloody feathers of slain birds, playing bridge with puffy pink-nailed jeweled fingers, women who after much expenditure of labor and bad temper still grotesquely resemble their own flatulent lap-dogs." He described a group of small-town citizens as a "Sunday-afternoon mob staring at monkeys in the

Zoo, poking fingers and making faces and giggling at the resentment of the more dignified race." He described Gantry
as being like his watch, "large, thick, shiny, with a near-gold
case," and declared, "He was born to be a senator. He never
said anything important, and he always said it sonorously."
College teachers were, he said, "spending the rest of their
lives reading fifteenth-hand opinions, taking pleasant naps,
and drooling out to yawning students the anemic and wordy
bookishness which they called learning." Of a Mrs. Bogart, a
Good Influence, he wrote,

> Mrs. Bogart was not the acid type of Good Influence. She was
> the soft, damp, fat, sighing, indigestive, clinging, melan-
> choly, depressingly hopeful kind. There are in every large
> chicken-yard a number of old and indignant hens who re-
> semble Mrs. Bogart, and when they are served at Sunday
> noon dinner, as fricasseed chicken with thick dumplings,
> they keep up the resemblance.

Of course, this kind of invective leads very directly to caricature, in which the bad is exaggerated and the good reduced.
For example Carol in *Main Street* went calling on Mrs. Ly-
man Cass, and Lewis wrote that she

> pounced on . . . the hook-nosed consort of the owner of the
> flour-mill. Mrs. Cass's parlor belonged to the crammed-
> Victorian school. . . . It was furnished on two principles: First,
> everything must resemble something else. A rocker had a
> back like a lyre, a near-leather seat imitating tufted cloth,
> and arms like Scotch Presbyterian lions; with knobs, scrolls,
> shields, and shear-points on unexpected portions of the
> chair. The second principle of the crammed-Victorian school
> was that every inch of the interior must be filled with useless
> objects.

Lewis then gives a detailed and hilarious listing of the contents of the parlor. The intention and the result is caricature.

Another kind of exaggeration results from a literal-
minded reductio ad absurdum, as in the assertion that "the
Maker of a universe with stars a hundred thousand light-
years apart was interested, furious, and very personal about
it if a small boy played baseball on Sunday afternoon." Lewis
is a master of this kind of literal statement for satiric ends,
as in "In the spring of '18 he was one of the most courageous
defenders of the Midwest against the imminent invasion of
the Germans." Carol Kennicott observes, "The respectability
of the Gopher Prairies . . . is reinforced by vows of poverty
and chastity in the matter of knowledge. Except for a half
dozen in each town the citizens are proud of that achieve-

ment of ignorance which it is so easy to come by." In examining what religious training gave Gantry, Lewis said,

> Sunday School text cards! True, they were chiefly a medium of gambling, but as Elmer usually won the game (he was the first boy in Paris to own a genuine pair of loaded dice) he had plenty of them in his gallery, and they gave him a taste for gaudy robes, for marble columns and the purple-broidered palaces of kings, which was later to be of value in quickly habituating himself to the more decorative homes of vice.

DESCRIBING THE SMALL TOWN

One of the qualities of Lewis's work that is difficult to describe or analyze is the way in which he can take the speech of his people, weave it into a monologue or an address, and make of it a severe indictment of the speaker, and yet appear at no point to be exaggerating the normal talk of such men. For example, this monologue from *Babbitt:*

> Every small American town is trying to get population and modern ideals. And darn if a lot of 'em don't put it across! Somebody starts panning a rube crossroads, telling how he was there in 1900 and it consisted of one muddy street, count 'em, one, and nine hundred human clams. Well, you go back there in 1920, and you find pavements and a swell little hotel and a first-class ladies' ready-to-wear shop—real perfection, in fact! You don't want to just look at what these small towns are, you want to look at what they're aiming to become, and they all got an ambition that in the long run is going to make 'em the finest spots on earth—they all want to be just like Zenith!

As Edgar Johnson has observed, "Burlesque there is in Lewis, but when we try to put a finger on it, in Babbitt's speech before the Real Estate Board, Luke Dawson's opinions on labor unions, or 'Old Jud's' Y.M.C.A. evangelism, it is embarrassingly apt to melt away and turn into realism. Mainly it is a matter of proportion rather than detail."

Some of Lewis's satire results from extravagant exaggeration with a perfectly straight face. An example is the section on "Weeks" in Chapter XXI of *Arrowsmith:*

> If an aggressive, wide-awake, live-wire, and go-ahead church or chamber of commerce or charity desires to improve itself, which means to get more money, it calls in those few energetic spirits who run any city, and proclaims a Week. This consists of one month of committee meetings, a hundred columns of praise for the organization in the public prints, and finally a day or two on which athletic persons flatter inappreciative audiences in churches or cinema theaters, and

the prettiest girls in town have the pleasure of being allowed
to talk to male strangers on the street corners, apropos of giving them extremely undecorative tags in exchange for the
smallest sums which those strangers think they must pay if
they are to be considered gentlemen.

Lewis holds the Middle Western world up to Juvenalian [re-
ferring to the Roman satirist Juvenal] laughter, points with
unmistakable directness to its weaknesses and errors, and,
as satirists have always done, seems to hope that seeing itself in the steel mirror of his description will make it repent
and improve. Sometimes what he has to say is blunt and direct. In *Main Street* he declares of the small town:

> It is an unimaginatively standardized background, a slug-
> gishness of speech and manners, a rigid ruling of the spirit by
> the desire to appear respectable. It is contentment ... the con-
> tentment of the quiet dead, who are scornful of the living for
> their restless walking. It is negation canonized as the one
> positive virtue. It is the prohibition of happiness. It is slavery
> self-sought and self-defended. It is dullness made God.

> A savorless people, gulping tasteless food, and sitting after-
> ward, coatless, and thoughtless, in rocking-chairs prickly with
> inane decorations, listening to mechanical music, saying me-
> chanical things about the excellence of Ford automobiles, and
> viewing themselves as the greatest race in the world.

Here the outrage and anger are not masked, the comic
cushion is not present. The point of view that leads the narrator through his long attack on the people of the books is
present in red-faced anger. But such direct statement is unusual in Lewis.

Even at his most solemn moments, wit and the comic
spirit usually cloak his rage. In a statement that is almost a
declaration of faith for Lewis, he describes Martin Arrowsmith as preaching to himself "the loyalty of dissent, the
faith of being very doubtful, the gospel of not bawling
gospels, the wisdom of admitting the probable ignorance of
one's self and of everybody else, and the energetic accelera-
tion of a Movement for going very slow." In that series of
witty paradoxes on a most serious subject Lewis is very
much himself. If the paradox undercuts a little the seriousness of the portrait of Martin Arrowsmith, it enhances the
role that Lewis the narrator wants to play. If his form is
nearer essay than fiction, if his laughter is more embittered
and angry than exuberant or outgoing, if his view of men
and institutions is that of Juvenal and not [Roman satirist]

Horace—that is merely another way of saying that he is of the Middle West and its towns and Main Streets, and while satiric laughter is an anodyne for what he feels there, he wants it to be more than an analgesic; he wants it to be a specific for the disease that causes the pain. If, as Mark Schorer has said, "he gave us a vigorous, perhaps a unique thrust into the imagination of ourselves," he intended the thrust to be therapeutic. If it has not been, then we are the poorer for its failure.

Aldous Huxley's *Brave New World* as an Anti-Utopian Satire

Stephen Jay Greenblatt

Brave New World by Aldous Huxley is one of the most well known anti-utopian satires. Stephen Jay Greenblatt asserts that Huxley has depicted a future in which passion and other human emotions have been replaced by a forced and sterile happiness. The sufferings and eventual suicide of his character known as the Savage show how traditional notions of humanity are unable to survive in a purported utopia. Greenblatt concludes that *Brave New World* is Huxley's darkest and most pessimistic novel. Greenblatt is a professor of English at the University of California at Berkeley and a former recipient of a Fulbright scholarship and Guggenheim fellowship.

Although all of his fiction has strong ironic elements, Aldous Huxley did not write satire exclusively, and his next truly satirical novel [after *Antic Hay*] is not, I believe, *Those Barren Leaves* (1925) or the long, semi-autobiographical *Point Counter Point* (1928), but *Brave New World* (1932), published almost ten years after *Antic Hay*. Huxley has stated that a utopian novel by H.G. Wells was the motivation for *Brave New World;* but it is obvious that the dangers of scientific materialism, blind faith in progress, and hedonism had long been troubling him, and his concern finally found full expression in this fine novel. In *Brave New World* Huxley has managed to sustain a structural simplicity and dynamism he sorely lacked in earlier works. He has also divested himself of the aura of the Jazz Age that has rather dated the novels of the 1920s, while retaining all of his standard devices of irony and satire—the contrapuntal themes, the dizzy piling

Excerpted from *Three Modern Satirists: Waugh, Orwell, and Huxley* by Stephen Jay Greenblatt, (New Haven, CT: Yale University Press, 1965). Copyright © 1965 by Stephen Jay Greenblatt. Reprinted with permission.

up of arguments and incidents, the witty caricatures. More important, working in a definite framework—the utopian novel—he is able to integrate fully his great talent for fantasy which he exhibited in "The History of Crome Manor" and his brilliant and bitter social criticism.

Point Counter Point is prefaced with lines by [Fulke] Greville which express the basic problem of all of Huxley's characters:

> O, wearisome conditions of humanity!
> Born under one law, to another bound,
> Vainly begot and yet forbidden vanity:
> Created sick, commanded to be sound.
> What meaneth Nature by these diverse laws—
> Passion and reason, self-division's cause?

In *Brave New World* this self-division is allegorized and forced to its ultimate conclusions. The realms of reason and passion are totally apart in Huxley's utopia, passion having been vanquished and exiled to a few remote, forbidding corners of the world. It is important to note that passion, for Huxley, is not necessarily or even probably gratification and pleasure, physical or otherwise. Rather, it is a sort of primal, *natural* emotion, which man experiences when he achieves profound union with nature. It is also important to see that *Brave New World*, like Orwell's *1984*, is primarily concerned not with what will happen in the future but what is happening to mankind now. A futuristic detail like the hatching of babies from bottles, for example, is less an interesting scientific speculation than an ironic comment on the dissociation of sexuality and childbirth and on the ultimate artificiality of the inhabitants of our brave new world.

HAPPINESS WITHOUT FREE WILL

The principles of reason, as seen by Huxley, are embodied in the Brave New World that is the realization of Mr. Scogan's "Rational State."[1] The basic goal of this state is the happiness of all, even if this happiness is purchased at the cost of imagination, discovery, free will, poetry, and pure science. The Trinity of the world state is "Community, Identity, Stability," and to achieve these ends, life is totally planned, *ab ovo* ["from the egg"]. Citizens of this "last word in organized good times and of secular revolutions" [according to Sisirkumar

---

1. Mr. Scogan was a character in Huxley's 1922 novel *Crome Yellow.*

Ghose] are hatched from bottles and predetermined as members of a strictly defined caste—alpha, beta, gamma, delta, or epsilon. Women undergo an "Operation . . . voluntarily for the good of Society, not to mention the fact that it carries a bonus amounting to six months' salary," and the remarkable "Bokanovsky's Process" successfully produces "scores of standard men and women from the same ovary and with gametes of the same male." By means of mass suggestion during sleep and other devious psychological techniques, the children are completely reconciled to their own caste and are given a strong aversion for beauty, art, and solitude. In their place are endless rounds of promiscuity and meaningless games, as well as "liquid air, television, vibro-vacuum massage, radio, boiling caffeine solution, hot contraceptives, and eight different kinds of scent . . . in every bedroom." The creatures of this world are doomed to be happy. No other kind of life is possible or imaginable. And if any vexations arise—like the mention of the obscene word "mother" or the arousal of a passion—there are always the pregnancy substitutes, the V.P.S. ("Violent Passion Surrogate—the complete physiological equivalent of fear and rage. All the tonic effects of murdering Desdemona and being murdered by Othello without any of the inconveniences"), and of course, that most delightful of all wonder drugs, soma ("All the advantages of Christianity and alcohol; none of their defects."). Such is the state of the world in the year 623 After-Ford ("Our Ford—or Our Freud, as, for some inscrutable reason, he chose to call himself whenever he spoke of psychological matters" is the deity of the Rational State). Man, in using his reason to create the ultimate life of pleasure, has ceased to be man.

Into this realm of unceasing and sterile happiness comes the Savage, the natural-born son of Linda, an ex-beta-minus who was abandoned on an Indian Reservation by the man who was "having" her for the week end, and discovered by Bernard Marx, one of the rare deviants from the Fordian norm (rumored cause—"alcohol in his blood surrogate"). The Savage has many unheard-of qualities and strange habits—he quotes Shakespeare, actually *loves* his mother, is a romantic, and believes in God. Living on the reservation, he is also disease-ridden, unhappy, filthy, and masochistic. Brought to London by Bernard, the Indian is a sensation among the fun-loving and curious citizens, but unfortunately the Savage's reaction to the Brave New World is not as favorable. He refuses to take soma, is not impressed by the titillating entertainments, and retches violently at the sight of the great numbers of mindless and identical creatures. Disgusted and desperate, the Savage flees to a lonely lighthouse and seeks solitude and self-punishment, but he is hounded unmercifully—yet without malice—by curiosity seekers and "feelie" makers and is finally driven to suicide.

In the last scene of the novel, the Savage's lifeless body hangs in the lighthouse and, turning slowly, sightlessly gazes on a world in which creativity, love, and God have been crushed by the weight of human happiness:

> Slowly, very slowly, like two unhurried compass needles, the feet turned towards the right; north, northeast, east, southeast, south, south-south-west; then paused, and, after a few seconds, turned as unhurriedly back towards the left. South-south-west, south, southeast, east.

CHARACTERIZATIONS IN *BRAVE NEW WORLD*

In *Brave New World* the few true human beings who have managed to resist Progress are deviants from the majority of society. Bernard Marx, Helmholtz Watson, and the Savage are all oddities in a world where the average man can't stand to be alone, blushes at the word "mother," and goes through life reciting the slogans which are, in fact, his total being. It is clearly not possible to be human and part of the system at the same time, for the essence of man is seen by Huxley as creativity, free will, recovery of natural passion, and these are heresies which the Brave New World has suppressed. The only member of the establishment who has remained human is Mustapha Mond, the world-controller, who, with a thorough knowledge of society both before and after Ford, freely chooses to side with the state and helps mold it with a brilliant but perverse creativity.

Bernard Marx is an unusual characterization in Huxley, for he is not a typed and static figure. Gradually, Huxley induces a shift in the reader's attitude toward Marx, from a thorough sympathy at the beginning of the novel to a scornful disdain at the close. Marx appeals to the reader at first because he does not fit into the Brave New World, but Bernard himself would very much like to be part of his society—to have the most pneumatic women, to be admired by the other alphas and feared by the lower castes. Unfortunately, a mistake during his hatching has made him smaller than average, neurotic, and maladjusted. Marx's intellectualism, his professed scorn for the values of his society are motivated not by an insight into the meaning of truth and beauty but by a hasty reaction formation to his alienation from the Brave New World. He loses the reader's sympathy when he uses the Savage as a device to gain attention. From this moment on, he diminishes from heroic to comic proportions and is finally revealed as a coward, begging to be allowed to stay in London rather than be sent to an island of misfits.

Helmholtz Watson, Bernard's friend, is a much more sympathetic character but remains a minor figure. If developed further, Watson could have been the successful alternative to the irreconcilable Savage and Mustapha Mond, as the person who finds meaning in creativity and poetry. But Watson is apparently introduced into the novel only to point out the decline of art into "emotional engineering" and the impossibility of free expression in the Brave New World.

Lenina Crowne, a pneumatic alpha whom the Savage at first adores as a goddess and a symbol of ultimate beauty, is generally a comic figure but with some tragic overtones. The reader senses that the ability to experience passion lies dormant within Lenina, but she has been trained to experience only mechanical, "rational" responses and does not have the imagination to transcend them. To the Savage's poetic ardors she can only respond with the words of a popular song, "Hug me till you drug me, honey."

THE IRRESOLVABLE CONFLICT

Brave New World is a remarkable novel and, in many respects, the culmination of Huxley's art. The gruesome utopian vision, presented in marvelous detail and with awesome imaginativeness, holds the reader in horrified fascination. Huxley has escaped from his self-conscious pedantry, his uncertainty, his lapses in style, and writes with boldness and assurance. *Crome Yellow* and *Antic Hay* had been seriously marred by a lack of dramatic tension, but *Brave New World* manages to achieve such tension through the direct confrontation of equally powerful, conflicting philosophies. Unlike the earlier novels, there is a very real debate in *Brave New World,* and, interestingly enough, the outcome of the debate as presented within the novel is a grim stalemate.

Near the end of the novel, the Savage and the World-Controller, Mustapha Mond, have a crucial argument. Mond

was a brilliant theoretical physicist with a knowledge of the
Bible, literature, and philosophy; but given a choice to be
sent to an island where he could continue his research or to
be taken on to the Controllers' Council, he chose the latter
and abandons the research. On the assumption that the happiness and stability of man are the only ultimate ends, all
troubling qualities which upset men such as truth, beauty,
love, knowledge, pure science *are* dangers and must be suppressed. "God isn't compatible with machinery and scientific medicine and universal happiness," Mond argues. The
poetic Savage, who mortifies his flesh and worships a stern
and terrible God, does not view this happiness and content-
ment as man's end. "What you need," he says to the World-
Controller, "is something with tears for a change. Nothing
costs enough here." Mustapha Mond astutely observes that
the Savage is "claiming the right to be unhappy." When the
Savage agrees defiantly, Mond goes on:

> "Not to mention the right to grow old and ugly and impotent;
> the right to have syphilis and cancer; the right to be lousy; the
> right to live in constant apprehension of what may happen to-
> morrow; the right to catch typhoid; the right to be tortured by
> unspeakable pains of every kind."

> "There was a long silence.

> "I claim them all," said the Savage at last.

> Mustapha Mond shrugged his shoulders, "You're welcome,"
> he said.

Who has won the argument? Both men on their own terms,
and neither; for Huxley and the reader, caught in between the
conflicting claims of "passion and reason, self-division's
cause," are locked in an irresolvable conflict, an unbreak-
able stasis. Huxley is able to offer no solution, no reconcili-
ation, no alternative. D.H. Lawrence's notion of Noble Savagery, which Huxley had flirted with, and even the fusion
with nature he had claimed as man's ideal, must be rejected
in the terms of *Brave New World.* Caught in the basic conflict
of the novel, they are torn apart and discredited. Half of the
creed resides with the closeness to nature and the savagery
of the Indian reservation but inextricably is mingled there
with disease, guilt, masochism, the hostile God. The other
half is found in the sexual release and rejection of abstrac-
tions of the Brave New World, but is likewise sullied by the
total dehumanization and absence of communication of its
inhabitants. *Brave New World* is the darkest point and final

stage of Huxley's pessimism. He is torn by irreconcilable views of man, and, admittedly [in his foreword to the novel], offers the reader the unenviable choice between "insanity on the one hand and lunacy on the other."

With *Brave New World*, Huxley ends the first and most productive period of his life. It is obvious, at the close of this novel, that the spiritual crisis in Huxley had reached its greatest intensity and could go no further. Sadly enough, the author could find no earthly solution. Rejecting this world entirely in bitterness and disgust, Huxley adopted the philosophy of nonattachment, a mystical belief of Buddhist origins, which leads man away from the ugliness of bodily existence and immerses him in eternal, changeless verities. Huxley did not cease writing satirical novels, but even the best of his later satires, *After Many a Summer Dies the Swan*, is marred by the spirit of a man who hates life and is sinning against it. The subtle irony, the surprise of a beautiful passage, the delicate portrayal of character have disappeared and are replaced by a ruthless and brutal hatred.

Huxley's dilemma was a conflict between a skeptical, sophisticated mind and essentially Victorian morals. His scientific outlook, the First World War, the disillusionment of the '20s—these destroyed intellectually the validity of all but relative moral standards, but emotionally, he was in desperate need of absolutes. It was as if the spirits of his two famous ancestors, T.H. Huxley and Matthew Arnold,[2] were locked in a mortal embrace in Huxley's soul. Huxley's tragedy is that of a man caught between two worlds, each with its own particular demands, truths, and horrors. Who can blame him for abandoning the struggle?

2. Thomas Henry Huxley was Aldous Huxley's grandfather and a biologist. Matthew Arnold was a poet and Aldous Huxley's great-uncle.

The Political Satire of George Orwell's *Animal Farm*

Jeffrey Meyers

In the following selection, Jeffrey Meyers asserts that George Orwell's novel *Animal Farm* is a satire of the Russian Revolution and subsequent communist takeover of that nation. Meyers shows how the characters in the novel parallel figures such as Joseph Stalin and Leon Trotsky and the ways in which the events in *Animal Farm*—such as the death of the horse Boxer and the accusations against the pig Snowball—parody grim realities in communist Russia. Meyers concludes that the political allegory of *Animal Farm* makes it a brilliant and courageous satire. Meyers is the editor of *George Orwell: The Critical Heritage* and the author of *Orwell: Wintry Conscience of a Generation* and *A Reader's Guide to George Orwell*, the book from which this article has been excerpted.

> The worker in his human functions no longer feels himself to be anything but animal. What is animal becomes human and what is human becomes animal.
>
> Karl Marx, *Economic and Philosophic Manuscripts of 1844*

Orwell believes that 'The business of making people *conscious* of what is happening outside their own small circle is one of the major problems of our time, and a new literary technique will have to be evolved to meet it.' His choice of a satiric beast fable for *Animal Farm* (1945) was exactly what he needed, for his creation of characters was always rather weak, and the flat symbolic animals of the fable did not have to be portrayed in depth. The familiar and affectionate tone

Excerpted from *A Reader's Guide to George Orwell* by Jeffrey Meyers (Totowa, NJ: Rowman and Allanheld, 1984). Copyright © 1975 Thames and Hudson, Ltd. Reprinted with permission.

of the story and its careful attention to detail allowed the unpopular theme to be pleasantly convincing, and the Soviet myth was exposed in a subtle fashion that could still be readily understood. It was written in clear and simple language that could be easily translated, and was short so that it could be sold cheaply and read quickly. The gay *genre* was a final attempt to deflect his profound pessimism, which dominated his final realistic vision of decency trampled on and destroyed in *1984*.

THE PURPOSE OF *ANIMAL FARM*

Experimentation with the literary techniques that could most forcefully convey his ideas is characteristic of all Orwell's non-fiction: autobiographical, sociological, and political. Though he had considerable success as a polemicist and pamphleteer, this *genre* was too blunt and too direct, for his views were extremely unpopular at the time he expressed them. *Animal Farm* was written [during WWII] between November 1943 and February 1944, after [the Russian victory at] Stalingrad and before [the U.S. and British invasion of] Normandy, when the Allies first became victorious and there was a strong feeling of solidarity with the Russians, who even in retreat had deflected Hitler from England. Distinguished writers like [H.G.] Wells, [George Bernard] Shaw, [Henri] Barbusse and [Romain] Rolland had praised Russia highly. But Orwell's book belongs with [Leon] Trotsky's *The Revolution Betrayed* (1937), [André] Gide's *Return From the U.S.S.R.* (1937) and [Arthur] Koestler's *Darkness At Noon* (1941), three prescient attacks on the Stalinist régime; and it anticipates post-war denunciations like [Richard] Crossman's compilation *The God That Failed* (1949) and [Milovan] Djilas' *The New Class* (1957).

Orwell had defined the theme of this book as early as 'Inside the Whale' (1940); and he writes in his essay on James Burnham (1946), 'History consists of a series of swindles, in which the masses are first lured into revolt by the promise of Utopia, and then, when they have done their job, enslaved over again by new masters.' In his Preface to the Ukrainian edition of *Animal Farm* (1947), he states that

> The man-hunts in Spain went on at the same time as the great purges in the USSR and were a sort of supplement to them. . . . Nothing has contributed so much to the corruption of the original idea of Socialism as the belief that Russia is a

Socialist country and that every act of its rulers must be ex-
cused, if not imitated. And so for the past ten years I have
been convinced that the destruction of the Soviet myth was
essential if we wanted a revival of the Socialist movement.

Orwell fused his artistic and political purpose so well that the
animals are completely convincing on the literal level. . . .

PARALLELS TO THE RUSSIAN REVOLUTION

'Comrade Napoleon', the poem of Minimus (who is based
on the poet [Vladimir Vladimirovich] Mayakovsky) is a
close imitation of adulatory Soviet verse like the 'Hymn to
J.V. Stalin':

The world has no person
Dearer, closer,
With him, happiness is happier,
And the sun brighter.
Friend of the fatherless!
Fountain of happiness!
Lord of the swill-bucket! Oh, how my soul is on
Fire when I gaze at thy
Calm and commanding eye,
Like the sun in the sky,
Comrade Napoleon!

And parts of the revolutionary song, 'Beasts of England',
closely paraphrase certain lines of 'L'Internationale' (1871):

C'est l' éruption de la fin
Soon or late the day is coming

Paix entre nous, guerre aux tyrans!
Tyrant Man shall be o'erthrown

La terre n'appartient qu'aux hommes
And the fruitful fields of England
Shall be trod by beasts alone.

Foule esclave, debout! Debout!
Rings shall vanish from our noses

Le soleil brillera toujours!
Bright will shine the fields of England.

'L'Internationale' expresses the brief but idealistic exhilara-
tion that Orwell experienced under the short-lived Anarchist
government in Barcelona. As he wrote to Cyril Connolly
from Spain in 1937, 'I have seen wonderful things & at last
really believe in Socialism, which I never did before.'

Immediately after the pigs celebrate their victory and bury
'some hams hanging in the kitchen' (a wonderful detail), the
revolutionary principles of Major are codified by Snowball

into 'The Seven Commandments' (which are reminiscent of the Five Chief Beatitudes of the Pukka Sahib in *Burmese Days*). The corruption inherent in the Rebellion is manifested as each of the Commandments is successively betrayed, until none of the original revolutionary idealism remains. As in Orwell's early novels and *1984*, the structure of the book is circular, and by the time the name is changed back to Manor Farm, there has been a return to the *status quo* (or worse) with whiskey and whips in the trotters of the pigs.

In the Preface to *Animal Farm*, Orwell writes: 'Although various episodes are taken from the actual history of the Russian Revolution, they are dealt with schematically and their chronological order is changed.' Thus, the human beings are capitalists, the animals are Communists, the wild creatures who could not be tamed and 'continued to behave very much as before' are the *muzhiks* or peasants, the pigs are the Bolsheviks, the Rebellion is the October Revolution, the neighbouring farmers are the western armies who attempted to support the Czarists against the Reds, the wave of rebelliousness that ran through the countryside afterwards is the abortive revolutions in Hungary and Germany in 1919 and 1923, the hoof and horn is the hammer and sickle, the Spontaneous Demonstration is the May Day celebration, the Order of the Green Banner is the Order of Lenin, the special pig committee presided over by Napoleon is the Politbureau, the revolt of the hens—the *first* rebellion since the expulsion of Jones (the Czar)—is the sailors' rebellion at the Kronstadt naval base in 1921, and Napoleon's dealings with Whymper and the Willingdon markets represent the Treaty of Rapallo, signed with Germany in 1922, which ended the capitalists' boycott of Soviet Russia.

THE MEANINGS OF CHARACTERS' NAMES

The carefully chosen names are both realistic and highly suggestive of their owners' personalities and roles in the fable. The imperious Major (Marx-Lenin) is military, dominant and senior (in public school jargon); the rather stupid and self-sacrificing Boxer (the proletariat), who is contrasted to the cynical Benjamin and the indifferent and unenthusiastic cat, is named after the Chinese revolutionaries who drove out foreign exploiters and were themselves crushed; Mollie (the White Russians) suggests folly, and her retrogressive defection for vanity and luxury is a paradigm of the entire revolution; Moses (the Russian Orthodox and later the Catholic Church) brings divine law to man; Squealer (a living *Pravda* [Soviet newspaper]) is ono-matopoetic for a voluble pig; and Whymper, the pigs' agent, suggests a toady. Pilkington (Churchill-England), the capitalist exploiter, connotes 'bilk' and 'milk' (slang): he is an old-fashioned gentleman who enjoys country sports on Foxwood, which has associations of both craftiness and the Tory landed gentry. Frederick (Hitler) refers to Frederick the Great, the founder of the Prussian military state and Hitler's hero. Frederick is a tough, shrewd man who drives hard bargains, steals other people's land for his own farm, Pinchfield, and practices terrible cruelties upon his subjects. These cruelties are related to the most moving scene in the novel—when Boxer is taken to the slaughter-house—for the knacker's van recalls the terrible gas vans used by the *Einsatzgruppen*[1] for mobile extermination. Though Clover screams out, 'They are taking you to your death,' the sound of Boxer's drumming hoofs inside the van 'grew fainter and died away'.

The most important animals are Napoleon (Stalin) and Snowball (Trotsky), whose personalities are antithetical and who are never in agreement. Both characters are drawn fully and accurately, though with simple strokes, and reflect almost all the dominant characteristics of their historical models. Like Trotsky, Orwell compares Stalin to Napoleon, for both turned revolutions into dictatorships . . . both transformed a national popular 'revolution from below' into a foreign conqueror's 'revolution from above', and both forcibly imposed their revolutionary ideology on other countries. Napoleon the pig is fierce-looking, 'not much of a talker, but with a reputation for getting his own way'. He dominates the party machinery, controls the education of the young and is superb at plotting and 'canvassing support for himself' between meetings. Napoleon never presents any of his own plans and always criticizes Snowball's, though he eventually adopts these plans and even claims he invented them. He first distorts and then changes history, blames Snowball for all his own failures, accuses him of plotting with foreign enemies, drives him into exile and finally pro-

1. *Einsatzgruppen* were mobile killing units operated by the Security Service which accompanied Germany into the Soviet Union and, often with the assistance of local police, shot 1.25 million Jews and other Soviet nationals.

nounces his death sentence. He also publishes fantastic production figures, takes 'credit for every successful achievement and every stroke of good fortune', wins elections unanimously, names cities after himself and replaces the cult of Major ('the animals were required to file past the skull [Lenin's Tomb] in a reverent manner') with a more elaborate one of his own. As Orwell writes in 1941, 'One could not have a better example of the moral and emotional shallowness of our time, than the fact that we are now all more or less pro-Stalin. This disgusting murderer is temporarily on our side, and so the purges etc. are suddenly forgotten.'

The name Snowball recalls Trotsky's white hair and beard, and the fact that he melted before Stalin's opposition. Snowball is a brilliant speaker, sometimes unintelligible to the masses but always eloquent and impressive, more vivacious and inventive than Napoleon, and a much greater writer. He is also intellectual and energetic. For, as [Isaac] Deutscher writes of Trotsky in 1921, besides running the army and serving on the Politbureau,

> He was busy with a host of other assignments each of which would have made a full-time job for any man of less vitality and ability. He led, for instance, the Society of the Godless. . . . He was at this time Russia's chief intellectual inspirer and leading literary critic. He frequently addressed audiences.

Orwell's description of Snowball's activities, though a comic parody, is close to reality:

> Snowball also busied himself with organising the other animals into what he called Animal Committees. . . . He formed the Egg Production Committee for the hens, the Clean Tails League for the cows, the Wild Comrades Re-education Committee . . . and various others, besides instituting classes in reading and writing.

Snowball studies military history, organizes, commands and leads the Army to victory in the Battle of the Cowshed (the Civil War) where foreign powers help Mr Jones and invade the farm (Russia). After the War he was 'full of plans for innovations and improvements'.

ANIMAL FARM AS AN ALLEGORY

Two of the most important battles between Trotsky and Stalin are allegorized in the novel. Trotsky fought for the priority of manufacturing over agriculture and for accelerated industrialization, and his ideas for the expansion of the Socialist sector of the economy were eventually adopted by

Stalin in the first five-year plan of 1928, which called for collectivization of farms *and* for industrialization: 'Snowball
conjured up pictures of fantastic machines which would do
their work for them while they grazed at their ease in the
fields . . . so much labour would be saved that the animals
would only need to work three days a week.' Stalin wanted
comprehensive and drastic collectivization: Napoleon 'argued that the great need of the moment was to increase food
production, and that if they wasted time on the windmill
they would all starve to death'.

In their central ideological conflict, Trotsky defended his
idea of 'Permanent Revolution' against Stalin's theory of 'Socialism in One Country'. Deutscher writes that 'Two rival
and quasi-Messianic beliefs seemed pitted against one another: Trotskyism with its faith in the revolutionary vocation
of the proletariat of the West; and Stalinism with its glorification of Russia's socialist destiny.' Orwell presents this con-
troversy in simpler but entirely accurate words:

> According to Napoleon, what the animals must do was to pro-
> cure firearms and train themselves in the use of them. Ac-
> cording to Snowball, they must send out more and more pi-
> geons and stir up rebellion among the animals on the other
> farms. The one argued that if they·could not defend them-
> selves they were bound to be conquered, the other argued
> that if rebellions happened everywhere they would have no
> need to defend themselves.

When Snowball comes to the crucial points in his speeches,
'It was noticed that [the sheep] were especially liable to
break into "Four legs good, two legs bad",' just as in the
party Congress in 1927, at Stalin's instigation, 'pleas for the
opposition were drowned in the continual, hysterically in-
tolerant uproar from the floor'. The Trotsky-Stalin conflict
reached a crucial point in mid-1927, after Britain broke
diplomatic relations with Russia and ruined Stalin's hopes
for an agreement between Soviet and British trade unions;
the Russian ambassador to Poland was assassinated; and
Chiang Kai-shek massacred the Chinese Communists who
had joined him at Stalin's orders. Trotsky and the Opposition
issued a declaration attacking Stalin for these political and
military failures, but before they could bring this issue before the party Congress and remove Stalin from power, he
expelled Trotsky and [Gregory] Zinoviev from the Party. Orwell writes of this vital moment in Soviet history, which sig-

nalled the final defeat of Trotsky, 'By the time he [Snowball] had finished speaking, there was no doubt as to the way the vote would go. But just at this moment' Napoleon's dogs (the GPU, or Secret Police) attacked Snowball and forced him to flee the farm and go into exile.

Orwell is not primarily interested in the practical or ideological merits of these controversies, for he believed (wrongly, I think) that *both* men had betrayed the revolution. He told a friend that 'Trotsky-Snowball was potentially as big a villain as Stalin-Napoleon, although he was Napoleon's victim. The first note of corruption was struck when the pigs secretly had the cows' milk added to their own mash and Snowball consented to this first act of inequity.' And he writes in 1939, the year before Trotsky's murder, 'It is probably a good thing for Lenin's reputation that he died so early. Trotsky, in exile, denounces the Russian dictatorship, but he is probably as much responsible for it as any man now living, and there is no certainty that as a dictator he would be preferable to Stalin, though undoubtedly he has a much more interesting mind.'

The three main Russian political events that are most extensively allegorized in *Animal Farm* are the disastrous results of Stalin's forced collectivization (1929–33) the Great Purge Trials (1936–38)[2] and the diplomacy with Germany that terminated with Hitler's invasion in 1941. Orwell writes that 'after Snowball's expulsion, the animals were somewhat surprised to hear Napoleon announce that the windmill was to be built after all'. The first demolition of the windmill, which Napoleon blames on Snowball, is the failure of the first five-year plan. The destructive methods of the hens during the 'Kronstadt Rebellion'—they 'made a determined effort to thwart Napoleon's wishes. Their method was to fly up to the rafters and there lay their eggs, which smashed to pieces on the floor'—are precisely those used by the *muzhiks* [Russian peasants] in 1929 to protest against the forced collectivization of their farms: 'In desperation they slaughtered their cattle, smashed implements, and burned crops. This was the *muzhiks'* great Luddite-like rebellion.' The result of this enormous ruin was, as Orwell writes in a 1938 review of

2. These were a series of trials that were held in the Soviet Union in the late 1930s. In these trials, many important Old Bolsheviks were found guilty of treason, based solely on their confessions and preliminary examinations, and either imprisoned or executed. However, it was later discovered that the cases had been fabricated and that the alleged criminals were innocent and had made confessions under duress.

[Eugene] Lyons's book on Russia [*Assignment in Utopia*], 'years of appalling hardship, culminating in the Ukraine famine of 1933, in which a number estimated at not less than three million people starved to death.' Deutscher mentions the recurrent cannibalism during times of starvation, and Orwell refers to this famine when he writes, 'It was being put about that all the animals were dying of famine and disease . . . and had resorted to cannibalism and infanticide.'

THE TRIALS

The most dramatic and emotional political events of the thirties were the Great Purge Trials, the minute details of which were published in the official translation of 1938. Stalin's motive, according to the editors of the trial's transcript, was a craving 'to achieve an unrestricted personal dictatorship with a totality of power that he did not yet possess in 1934'. They also state that in the trial 'pieces of falsified real history have been woven along with outright fiction'. A perfect example of this occurs when the animals 'remembered that at the critical moment of the battle Snowball had turned to flee', but forgot that it was a deliberate ruse to prepare the victorious ambush.

In the trial of Trotsky's friend Karl Radek, in February 1937, the prosecution claimed that Trotsky

was organizing and directing industrial sabotage in the Soviet Union, catastrophes in coal mines, factories, and on the railways, mass poisonings of Soviet workers, and repeated attempts on the lives of Stalin and other members of the Politbureau.

After the destruction of the windmill, Napoleon roars:

thinking to set back our plans . . . this traitor has crept here under cover of night and destroyed our work of nearly a year. . . .

A rumour went round that Snowball had after all contrived to introduce poison into Napoleon's food.

In the last and most important trial, that of Bukharin in March 1938, Gorky's secretary Kryuchkov confessed, 'I arranged long walks for Alexei Maximovich, I was always arranging bonfires. The smoke of the bonfire naturally affected Gorky's weak lungs.' During the purge in *Animal Farm*, 'Two other sheep confessed to having murdered an old ram, an especially devoted follower of Napoleon, by chasing him round and round a bonfire when he was suffering from a cough.'

In his review of Lyons's book, Orwell is horrified by the

'monstrous state trials at which people who have been in prison for months or years are suddenly dragged forth to make incredible confessions', and, in his satire, 'A sheep confessed to having urinated in the drinking pool—urged to do this, so she said, by Snowball.' Tucker and Cohen state that nine million people were arrested during the purges, and that the number of people executed has been reliably estimated at three million. In *Animal Farm,* all the 'guilty' animals are 'slain on the spot', and in a terrifying moment of the book, after the confessions and executions, 'there was a pile of corpses lying before Napoleon's feet and the air was heavy with the smell of blood'.

After solidifying his domestic power through massive liquidation, Stalin turned his attention to the increasing menace in Europe and attempted to play off the democracies against Hitler. Deutscher describes how

> He still kept his front doors open for the British and the French and confined the contact with the Germans to the back stairs. . . . It is still impossible to say confidently to which part of the game Stalin then attached the greatest importance: to the plot acted on the stage or to the subtle counter-plot.

Similarly, the animals were amazed when they discovered that, during Napoleon's apparent friendship with Pilkington, he 'had really been in secret agreement with Frederick'. But Napoleon is sadly deceived: Frederick's bank notes (the Hitler-Stalin non-aggression pact of August 1939) are forgeries, and he attacks Animal Farm without warning and destroys the windmill. . . .

A COMPLETE AND ACCURATE SATIRE

The satire concludes, as Orwell says in the Preface, with the 1943 'Tehran Conference,'[3] which was taking place while I was writing.' Deutscher, who knew him, relates that Orwell was 'unshakably convinced that Stalin, Churchill, and Roosevelt consciously plotted to divide the world, and to divide it for good, among themselves, and to subjugate it in common. . . . "*They* are all power-hungry," he used to repeat.' The disagreement between the allies and the beginning of the cold war is symbolized when Napoleon and Pilkington,

---

3. Held November 28–December 1, 1943, in Tehran, Iran, it was a meeting between President Franklin D. Roosevelt, British Prime Minister Winston Churchill, and Soviet Premier Joseph Stalin to discuss the war and postwar political issues.

both suspicious, 'played an ace of spades simultaneously'.

The political allegory of *Animal Farm,* whether specific or general, detailed or allusive, is pervasive, thorough and accurate, and the brilliance of the book becomes much clearer when the satiric allegory is compared to the political actuality. Critics who write, 'it makes a delightful children's story' and who emphasize that 'the gaiety in his nature had completely taken charge' are dimly unaware of the allegory's sophisticated art. Orwell wrote to Middleton Murry the year he finished the work, 'I consider that willingness to criticise Russia and Stalin is *the* test of intellectual honesty,' and by his own or any standard it is an honest and even a courageous book.

CHAPTER 4

Responding to Satire

 Satire

Satire Causes Feelings of Uneasiness

Patricia Meyer Spacks

In the following essay, Patricia Meyer Spacks concludes that one of the most important responses to satire is uneasiness. This uneasiness is caused by the satirist's depiction of a universe that is filled with unresolved problems. An example Spacks provides of a satire that sparks considerable reader response is Jonathan Swift's essay "A Modest Proposal," which suggests that Ireland respond to its famine by selling its children as food. According to Spacks, the essay is discomforting not only because it recommends cannibalism, but also because it depicts the horrifying conditions in Ireland that prompted the narrator's grim solution. She concludes that while not all works of satire, such as Alexander Pope's "The Rape of the Lock," prompt an equally agonized response, no piece of literature can be considered true satire unless it leads to some level of uneasiness. Spacks is an Edgar F. Shannon Professor in eighteenth-century literature at the University of Virginia in Charlottesville and the author of several books, including *Desire and Truth: Functions of Plot in Eighteenth-Century English Novels.*

What, exactly, *is* the satiric emotion? The only critic I know of who has considered this problem is Gilbert Highet, who suggests [in *Anatomy of Satire*] that the satiric emotion combines amusement and contempt in varying proportions. "Hatred which is not simply shocked revulsion but is based on a moral judgment, together with a degree of amusement which may range anywhere between a sour grin at the incongruity of the human condition and a delighted roar of laughter at the exposure of an absurd fraud—such are, in

Excerpted from "Some Reflections on Satire," by Patricia Meyer Spacks, *Genre*, vol. 1, 1968. Copyright © 1968 by the author. Reprinted with permission.

varying proportions, the effects of satire. When they are absent from a piece of fiction, it is not satirical." This description does not seem adequate, however, to the works of [Jonathan] Swift: amusement is hardly a component of one's response to *A Modest Proposal*, and contempt is not an adequate description of what one actually feels. There are amusing monuments in the fourth book of [*Gulliver's Travels*], but its most powerful sections evoke neither amusement nor contempt. It is difficult to see, moreover, why these particular emotions, alone or in combination, should create any impulse toward action. Amusement is its own fulfillment; contempt, directed toward others, is satisfying in itself, with its implication of the scorner's superiority; directed toward the self, it produces despair.

SATIRE CAUSES DISCOMFORT

If satire sometimes generates self-satisfaction and complacency (when we can clearly identify its victims as other than ourselves), a more important satiric response is, I would suggest, uneasiness—the kind of uneasiness [playwright Bertolt] Brecht wished to induce in his audiences by refusing them the security and satisfaction of emotional release in the theater. In satire, as in the Brechtian theater, one is not allowed to identify with the characters; one does not *wish* to identify with them. The satiric plot, as Professor [Alvin] Kernan has demonstrated, does not provide the satisfaction of completion. The reader is left insecure, unanchored; if positive standards have been by implication reasserted, they have been shown as seriously threatened by reality. To resolve the insecurity, the revealed tension between *is* and *ought*, the reader must take—or plan, imagine, speculate about—action. The satirist does not give him any view of the universe which leads to exalted tragic or resigned comic acceptance. He depicts a universe full of unresolved problems. In the best satire he is likely to create level upon level of uneasiness; as our insight increases, we see ever more sharply our own involvement in tangles which it is our responsibility to unravel. In the most powerful satire, too, uneasiness plays constantly against complacency: we identify the victims as others and feel our superiority, only to find ourselves trapped a moment later, impaled by the scorn we have comfortably leveled against the rest of the world.

It has often been suggested that satire is not really possible in the twentieth century: either everything is satire or nothing is. Read a Sears Roebuck ad: "Newest U.S. M-16 Rifle Assault Weapon System. Complete set $4.88. Dash through the underbrush, toss cap-exploding grenade and trigger off cap-firing M-16 rifle. 30-inch rifle field strips to form 3 other weapons for sniping, covering fire or close combat. Caps store in clip, scope removes. When you can, sip water from canteen. You wear a jungle bush hat, dog tags, soft 9½-inch knife in leg sheath. Plastic and metal." In the context of a catalogue full of toys, this hardly gives us a pause: it describes a common artifact of our time. Isolated, taken out of context, it seems an attack on our corrupt values, an attack which works by grotesque exaggeration: satire. The difference between the two kinds of understanding of the same paragraph is a difference in emotional response. If we read the advertisement with no response other than a judgment of the toy's entertainment value, it has no satiric effect; [if] we respond with an uneasiness which leads immediately to social criticism, it seems satiric.

Obviously, we never really take the Sears Roebuck ad as satire because we are aware of the commercial intent which forms it. An advertisement is not a literary phenomenon and we do not judge it as one. But there is a serious point here. The language of the blurb, like the procedures of Forest Lawn Cemetery, could be put without further heightening into a satiric context; it would then generate satiric uneasiness; it would become in effect satire.

UNEASINESS AS A REACTION TO SWIFT

The importance of the psychic disturbance satire creates is of course clearest and most significant in works of satiric intent. Jonathan Swift's *Modest Proposal for Preventing the Children of Ireland from being a Burden to their Parents or Country* demonstrates how effective a satiric device is the generation and complex maneuvering of the reader's uneasiness. Swift works, here as in his other satiric writing, by exploiting various degrees of awareness in his readers. One's responses to the *Modest Proposal* are likely to proceed by an orderly heightening and deepening of emotion. First the speaker presents himself as a rational, practical man. He invites our participation in his concern for Ireland, the concern of a man aware of economic realities but full of feeling as well: the first words of the piece are, "It is a melancholly

Object . . ." We assume (I am trying to recapture the initial response to the essay: obviously a second or third reading contaminates the opening paragraphs with our knowledge of what is to come)—we assume that we are intended to identify with the speaker in his intent to make "these Children sound and useful Members of the Commonwealth," that the satiric target will be elsewhere. No uneasiness so far: everything seems set up to encourage our complacency at our ability to grasp social problems in larger and more meaningful terms than mere sentimentality.

We are not long allowed to remain in our state of self-satisfaction. The point at which we become suspicious of the speaker depends on the degree of our sensitivity. Is it at the end of the second paragraph, where his motivation seems connected with his desire to see his "Statue set up for a Preserver of the Nation"? Or in the fourth paragraph, where he refers to "a Child, *just dropt from its Dam*"? By the time we reach paragraph six, where the modest proposer treats stealing as an economic solution with no apparent awareness of any moral question associated with it, we are almost certain to have become nervous; the next paragraph, with its consideration of boys and girls as salable commodities, is positively disturbing. The suggestion that children be sold for food occurs shortly thereafter, making further identification with the speaker finally untenable.

For a moment, then, we are turned adrift. As our skepticism about the speaker's values increases, we must question our own values, which have earlier seemed to coincide with his. The speaker, we begin to feel, is the object of satire; and we, as readers, are implicated. But the resultant uneasiness soon yields to a new kind of complacency. At least now we realize more than the speaker does; we can judge him with the superiority of moralists, recognize and condemn his moral impoverishment, shudder at the barbarity which Swift's diction constantly calls to our attention.

But we are not yet secure. The next series of disturbing suggestions concerns the state of affairs the proposer's suggestions are designed to correct. First the speaker claims that cruelty "hath always been with me the strongest Objection against any Project, how well soever intended." Apparently he does not find his own proposal cruel. Why not? Perhaps we answer that he lacks self-knowledge, he does not realize what he is suggesting. But he goes on to describe the people, *"dying,* and *rotting,* by *Cold* and *Famine,* and *Filth,* and *Vermin"*; to suggest that his proposal will have the advantage that "Men would become as *fond* of their Wives, during the Time of their Pregnancy, as they are now of their *Mares* in Foal, their *Cows* in Calf, or *Sows* when they are ready to farrow; nor offer to beat or kick them, (as is too *frequent* a Practice) for fear of a Miscarriage"; to reveal that at present the poorer tenants own nothing, "their Corn and Cattle being already seized, and *Money a Thing Unknown.*" We begin to suspect what we only feel fully at the end of the essay: that the true horror is in the state of affairs that produces the proposal, not in the proposal itself, which comes to seem more and more dreadfully plausible. Is this cannibalism not, after all, quite rational; is it not, indeed, almost inevitable under the circumstances the projector so graphically and specifically describes? "I desire the Reader will observe," he writes, "that I calculate my Remedy *for this one individual Kingdom of Ireland, and for no other that ever was, is, or, I think, ever can be upon Earth.*" He has looked coolly at the facts of the situation; sheer rationality has led him to his solution. Centuries of traditional morality forbid us to take it seriously; still we become aware of its compelling logic. Since we cannot accept the logic we recognize, we face a new dilemma, a more radical source of uneasiness: rationality itself is being called into question. If rational thinking leads to barbarity, must we reject our commitment to it? Does our contempt for the speaker involve us in contempt for clear-headedness? Is our regard for morality mere sentimentality, and misguided sentimentality at that?

Once more, Swift rescues us: we do not have to remain in our uneasiness, we climb to a new level of security and shift from satiric uneasiness (we are implicated, we can't even understand quite how, we don't know how to get out) to satiric superiority with the list of solutions which the proposer declares to be impossible because the Irish people will not put them into practice. These solutions supply a refreshing note of sanity (they are solutions which Swift straightforwardly recommended elsewhere). We grasp at them eagerly, and note that they combine economic awareness with moral sensitivity. Shopkeepers are to have *"a Spirit of Honesty, Industry, and Skill"*; at present they treat their customers unfairly. Absentees should be taxed, local production utilized, pride, vanity and idleness cured: throughout the long list, economic solutions merge with moral ones. We realize now that the proposer possesses rationality but not reason in the eighteenth-century definition, which makes reason a moral as well as a rational faculty (cf. the fourth book of *Gulliver's Travels*). We have new grounds for feeling superior to the projector who fails by Swift's clear standards, with which we now gratefully align ourselves. But Swift is not yet through with us.

REJECTING THE PROPOSAL

A residue of uneasiness remains after the list of positive proposals because of the speaker's firm assurance that there is unlikely ever to be "some hearty and sincere Attempt to put *them in Practice.*" The standard of true reason is tempting, we cling to the assurance it provides, but perhaps it is irrelevant to the immediate situation. The nature of that situation suddenly becomes more vivid, in the next to the last paragraph of the essay. The projector seems to recognize the possibility of objections to his proposal, but he challenges anyone to find a counter-proposal "equally innocent, cheap, easy, and effectual." Anyone who offers another solution, he points out, must consider two points:

> First, as Things now stand, how they will be able to find Food and Raiment, for a Hundred Thousand useless Mouths and Backs? And *Secondly,* There being a round Million of Creatures in human Figure, throughout this Kingdom; whose whole Subsistence, put into a common Stock, would leave them in Debt two Millions of Pounds *Sterling;* adding those, who are Beggars by Profession, to the Bulk of Farmers, Cottagers and Labourers, with their Wives and Children, who are Beggars in Effect; I desire those Politicians, who dislike my Overture, and may perhaps be so bold to attempt an Answer, that they will first ask the Parents of these Mortals, Whether they would not at this Day think it a great Happiness to have been sold for Food at a Year old, in the Manner I prescribe; and thereby have avoided such a perpetual Scene of Misfortunes, as they have since gone through; by the *Oppression of Landlords;* the Impossibility of paying Rent, without Money or Trade; the Want of common Sustenance, with neither House nor Cloaths, to cover them from the Inclemencies of the Weather; and the most inevitable Prospect of intailing the like, or greater Miseries upon their Breed for ever.

This paragraph introduces no important new facts. With great economy and point, it reviews data previously presented, and it suggests—almost enforces—the cataclysmic shift of perspective hinted earlier. Through most of the essay we have felt secure in our superiority to the projector. If we waver briefly in our assurance about the grounds of our superiority, we proceed to the conviction that by the highest standards we can judge him and find him wanting. Now, though, his calm rationality suggests that he might with equal validity judge us and find us wanting. The people he describes would think it a happiness to be sold for food, to avoid the horrors of the life they live. The proposal that they be so sold is barbarous; the situation that might lead the victims to welcome it is worse. Most people, of course, accept the starvation, helplessness, hopelessness of masses of others with perfect equanimity. The modest proposer has offered an intolerable solution to an intolerable situation. We judge his solution inhuman, and condemn him for suggesting it. But if the situation is worse than the solution, if it is even equally bad, surely the people who accept it as the given state of affairs, who coolly evaluate solutions and reject proposals and proposals alike without themselves doing anything to alleviate the problem—surely such people must be condemned. And who are they? The piece becomes an indictment of the people of Ireland, who do nothing about their plight, and of the people of England, who do nothing either; and, like so much of Swift's work, it reaches out beyond its time and place to indict the twentieth-century reader who accepts as inevitable man's inhumanity to man, who rests secure in his reason and morality without involving himself in the horror of social inequity. Swift's positive standards include humanity as well as reason. If we take his essay seriously, allow ourselves to be affected by it, we are left in a state of profound uneasiness, recognizing our involvement in the evil to which we have earlier felt superior.

It is dangerous to try to specify what a reader's reaction will be to any work of art. There are readers and readers; there are even readers who remain unaffected by Swift's manipulations, who read *A Tale of a Tub* without questioning their own sanity or the standards by which they judge sanity, read the fourth book of *Gulliver* without wondering about their own self-satisfactions. One can only try to specify the effects the work of art seems to demand; and the most important effect demanded by the *Modest Proposal* is profound disturbance, achieved by the development of various levels of uneasiness and complacency. . . .

Uneasiness can be a gentle, almost a subliminal, emotion.

. . . But gentle satire is still satire, and mild uneasiness still uneasiness, as [Alexander] Pope pointed out in a letter concerned with *The Rape of the Lock,* most gentle of satires: "This whimsical piece of work, as I have now brought it up to my first design, is at once the most a satire, and the most inoffensive, of anything of mine. People who would rather it were let alone laugh at it, and seem heartily merry, at the same time that they are uneasy. 'Tis a sort of writing very like tickling."

Pope here suggests his awareness that uneasiness is the natural response to satire and that it can co-exist with responses very different in kind, and he hints that the co-existence of contradictory emotions in a reader may be an index of literary quality. The faint uneasiness created by *The Rape of the Lock* and the intense moral disturbance generated by *A Modest Proposal* indicate the polar possibilities of satiric response. On the other hand, a work that evokes no real uneasiness in the reader is in effect not a satire at all. It may at one time have been one: a case in point is [John] Dryden's *Mac Flecknoe,* which satiric theorists unaccountably tend to group with Pope's *Dunciad.* The two poems seem to me dramatically different. The *Dunciad,* like Dante's *Inferno* (a work which also has its moments of satiric intensity), impales and immortalizes the poet's personal enemies by giving them more than personal significance. Like Sporus, Atossa, Balaam in Pope's shorter satires, Bentley and Theobald and Clibber, even such minor characters as James Ralph, become emblematic of moral and intellectual failings which have existed in all times and places. Any twentieth-century reader of intellectual pretensions—surely any reader who has ever thought of himself as a critic—can hardly avoid feeling disturbed at the possibility, the probability, that he participates in the sins here so conclusively damned. One reads *Mac Flecknoe* with a kind of innocent joy. If it was ever true satire, if Shadwell ever seemed to exemplify faults beyond himself, it has become with the passage of time mere lampoon. Lampoon, to be sure, of the highest order: Dryden's wit, verve, inventiveness display his own superiority to the poetaster he mocks, demonstrate in action the value of true poetic power. The positive values of the poem survive; its target has shrunk. Although *Mac Flecknoe* may achieve a moral effect on its readers through its embodiment of its positive values, it works entirely through the response of complacency (we are not, thank God, such as Shadwell) without creating any real disturbance.

Or a work existing in a satiric borderland (the borders, as Northrop Frye has illustrated, are comedy and tragedy) may be satire for some readers, not for others. [Lewis Caroll's] *Alice in Wonderland* seems to some adults an entertaining fantasy with Freudian overtones. Others find it a satiric attack on the values, assumptions and procedures of the adult world which reveals the hypocrisy, arbitrariness and cruelty of that world through the eyes of a child. Alice's curious versions of the poems she has been taught frequently embody the true as opposed to the professed values of the world in which she is growing up. The adult reader perceptive of satiric nuance finds himself implicated, sees himself as almost one of the mythical creatures surrounding Alice. He may be more disturbed than Lewis Carroll could have intended by the fact that the positive standards of the satire are contained in the idea of childish innocence, a state which can only be yearned for and regretted, never re-achieved. In its romantic image of the child (this despite the fact that it demonstrates awareness of the child's potentiality for cruelty, unfairness, thoughtlessness) *Alice in Wonderland* seems a typical nineteenth-century product; yet in its satiric implications it foreshadows the despair characteristic of twentieth-century satire, which exposes a corrupt world, demonstrates the power of intelligence in understanding the evil which surrounds us, but offers no hope of significant change.

NEW DIRECTIONS FOR SATIRE

Some twentieth-century satire attempts too easy a way. Barbara Garson's *Mac Bird* has been hailed in some quarters as brilliant contemporary satire. The response it evokes, it seems to me, is complacency without uneasiness: in other words, it lacks the perceptual complexity of true satire. Certainly it begins with a clever, if rather collegiate, idea, the notion that light can be shed on our current political corruption by placing it in a Shakespearean context. The implementation of the idea does not equal the conception. The author seems out of control of her material, unable even to manipulate the plot so that it says what she wants to say. (She has published several disclaimers of any serious intent to suggest that President Johnson was involved in the assassination of President Kennedy.) Her ear for verse rhythms is crude, her sense of humor obvious; the play contains no real surprises and achieves no authority. Those who admire it tend to be those who share the political convictions from which it derives. They find it a satisfying attack on the enemy. In no way are they involved or judged or questioned by the action or the language; if the play causes in them uneasiness about the state of the nation, this is not the satiric kind of uneasiness. Mrs. Garson's effort is likely to generate only self-satisfaction in its admirers. For those who do not share the play's political stance it seems tasteless or irrelevant or both. It enforces no new awareness; it asserts, rather than engineers assent. In order to evoke uneasiness, satire must be convincing, or at least compelling. This kind of pseudo-satire—it is really burlesque or travesty—convinces only those who are convinced already. It lacks the genuine satiric tickle.

Mac Bird is by no means representative of twentieth-century satiric achievement; I have discussed it only because its critical reception suggests some questions about the response to satire. More interesting directions for satire emerge in the political allegories of Huxley and Orwell; the social commentary of early Waugh, early Kingsley Amis, late Anthony Burgess; the verse of W.H. Auden and Robert Lowell (whose version of Juvenal's *Vanity of Human Wishes* exemplifies vital differences between classical and modern conceptions of satire's function); the science fiction of Kurt Vonnegut, Jr.; the songs of Tom Lehrer, the skits of Mike Nichols and Elaine May, of [Michael] Flanders and [Donald] Swann. All these works appeal to a limited audience, if only because none but limited groups now hold standards in common. All involve their audiences in a special tension of perception, encourage complacent superiority only to shatter it, tease the onlooker until he does not know whether he feels pleasure or pain. Such has always been the special achievement of satire.

The Defense of Satirists

Robert C. Elliott

Satirists face perhaps more criticism than any other
group of writers. In the following selection, Robert C.
Elliott details the ways in which satirists have defended their work. Among the more common defenses are apologia, in which satirists assert that they
are writing because they are disgusted by the evil
that surrounds them. In these apologies, the satirists
often display conservatism and a wish to strengthen
the established order. However, the apologies do not
always silence those who oppose satire on the
grounds that it is immoral and cruel, and while
satirists may claim to be conservative, their works often contain revolutionary ideas that society cannot
wholly approve or understand. Elliott was a founding
member of the department of literature at the University of California at San Diego and the author of several books, including *The Shape of Utopia: Studies in
a Literary Genre* and *The Power of Satire: Magic, Ritual, and Art,* the source of the following essay.

We have an excellent opportunity to examine the satirist's
claims for social approval largely by reason of the literary
convention which decrees that he must justify his ungrateful art. From the times of [Roman satirists] Horace, Persius,
and Juvenal, down to [French poet Nicolas] Boileau,
[Jonathan] Swift, and [Alexander] Pope, and into our own
day with men like Wyndham Lewis, the satirist has felt com-
pelled to write an *apologia,* whether formal or informal, in
verse or prose. The *apologiae* are remarkably similar in
their protestations (Mr. Lewis dissenting in part); from them
we get an ideal image which the satirist projects of himself
and his art. According to the image the satirist is a public
servant fighting the good fight against vice and folly wherever he meets it; he is honest, brave, protected by the recti-

Excerpted from *The Power of Satire: Magic, Ritual, and Art* by Robert C. Elliott
(Princeton, NJ: Princeton University Press, 1960). Copyright © 1960 Robert C. Elliott.

tude of his motives; he attacks only the wicked and then seldom or never by name; he is, in short, a moral man appalled by the evil he sees around him, and he is forced by his conscience to write satire. Juvenal's *facit indignatio versum* ["The indignation makes the verse"] is the prototype.

SATIRICAL DEFENSE AND SOCIETAL RESPONSE

The satirist claims, with much justification, to be a true conservative. Usually (but not always—there are significant exceptions) he operates within the established framework of society, accepting its norms, appealing to reason (or to what his society accepts as rational) as the standard against which to judge the folly he sees. He is the preserver of tradition, the true tradition from which there has been grievous falling away.

Society, quite naturally, is dubious. On the most obvious level it points to the inevitable discrepancy between the ideal image, projected by rhetorical convention, and what it takes to be the actual fact. Swift, or Pope—so goes the reasoning— was a wicked man; therefore we may dismiss his satire. The *non sequitur* is comforting. But the problem on other levels is more complex. Despite society's doubts about the character of the satirist, there may develop a feeling that in its general application his work has some truth in it—or the feeling that other people may *think* that it has some truth in it. Individuals who recognize characteristics of themselves in the objects of attack cannot afford to acknowledge the identity even privately. So they may reward the satirist as proof of piety, while inwardly they fear him. *"Satyr,"* says Swift in a passage quoted earlier, *"is a sort of Glass, wherein Beholders do generally discover every body's Face but their Own; which is the chief Reason for that kind Reception it meets in the World, and that so very few are offended with it."* "Publicly offended," one might add. Publicly the satirist may be honored, but privately he will be feared.

From the beginning satirists have been uneasily explicit about the antagonism they arouse. Each of the three major classical *apologiae* (Horace, II, 1; Persius, I; Juvenal, I) contains a warning from the interlocutor on the animosities stirred up by satire and on the dangers the satirist risks. The dangers are unquestionably real: satirists have always attacked vice and viciousness and stupidity as they exist in the real world, and they have had to face the antagonism that inevitably accompanies such activity. Countless satirists in all lands have been beaten, imprisoned, tortured, even executed as a result of their daring. During James I's reign a Pole named Stercovius wrote a harsh satire on the Scots. King James was furious. In 1609 he had passed an act with the consent of Parliament rigorously forbidding the issuance of "pasquillis, lybellis, rymes, cokalanis, commedies, and siclyk occasionis." Somehow, even though Stercovius was in Poland, James arranged to have him executed. The cost to the British government was six hundred pounds.

Even in periods when satire has flourished, opposition to it on moral and pragmatic grounds has been vigorous and outspoken. Gabriel Harvey, for example, writhing under the ridicule of [Robert] Greene, [Thomas] Nashe, and others, wrote in furious indignation against the outrage of satire: "Inuectiues by fauour haue bene too bolde: and Satyres by usurpation too-presumptuous: I ouerpasse *Archilochus, Aristophanes, Lucian, Iulian, Aretine,* and that whole venomous and viperous brood, of old & new Raylers: euen *Tully,* and *Horace* otherwhiles ouerreched. . . ." Yet in a bow to his enemies' abuse, Harvey says he will try to amend any defects with which he has justly been charged.

Sir William Temple felt that the popular vein of satire and ridicule (he uses the terms synonymously) was "the Itch of our Age and Clymat" and thoroughly noxious in effect. He cites with at least partial approval the theory of an ingenious Spaniard who held that *Don Quixote,* by subjecting the Spanish romantic attitudes toward love and valor to ridicule, had brought about the ruin of the Spanish monarchy. In England, Temple says, ridicule has "helpt to Corrupt our modern Poesy"; and while he can praise [François] Rabelais and [Miguel de] Cervantes, the great masters in this kind of writing, his final attitude is uncompromising: "But let the Execution be what it will, the Design, the Custom, and Example [of satire] are very pernicious to Poetry, and indeed to all Virtue and Good Qualities among Men, which must be disheartened by finding how unjustly and undistinguish't they fall under the lash of Raillery, and this Vein of Ridiculing the Good as well as the Ill, the Guilty and the Innocent together."

BAYLE'S ARGUMENT

The most strenuously articulate of all those who have written against satire on whatever grounds was Pierre Bayle, author of the influential *Dictionnaire historique et critique* (Rotterdam, 1697). For Bayle satire was the Art of Poisoning; in hundreds of passages in the *Dictionary* he lashes out at the immorality, the untruthfulness, the cruelty of satire, which, despite its protestations, he says, neither prevents crime nor effects reform. Bayle is clearly fascinated by what horrifies him. In the article on Hipponax he writes: "He was neither the first, nor the only person who have forced people to make away with themselves by their invectives." Then follows a long, long list of historical examples of those who are said to have died as a result of ridicule, vituperation, or reproach. Satire, libel, lampoon, defamation, slander, ridicule—all are one to Bayle, and the satirist no better than a "mad dog," whose motive is to kill: ". . . a satirist who attempts upon the honour of his enemy with libels, would attempt upon their life with sword or poison, if he had the same opportunity."

Bayle's arguments furnished ammunition for dozens of writers in the eighteenth century. Satirists were widely read and publicly applauded, but at the same time the distaste and fear which they inspired are plainly evident in the large body of literature directed against their mode. ". . . whence this Lust to Laugh?" queried William Whitehead lugubriously in his rhymed *Essay on Ridicule* (1743)—a plea for the demise of satire—and answered himself:

> Why, Shaftsb'ry tells us,
>   Mirth's the Test of Sense . . .
> Not so, fair Truth. . . .

Many echoed his "Not so." Dr. [Samuel] Johnson had no love for satire. In an allegorical essay in the *Rambler* he wrote that Satire, who was born of an unholy cohabitation of Wit and Malice, carried poisoned arrows which could never be extracted from his victims. Earlier, in a similar allegory, [Joseph] Addison had expressed his disapproval by characterizing satire as a woman with a smile on her face and a dagger concealed under her garment. William Cowper questioned satire's efficacy:

> Yet what can satire, whether grave or gay?
> It may correct a foible, may chastise
> The freaks of fashion, regulate the dress,
> Retrench a sword-blade, or displace a patch;
> But where are its sublimer trophies found?
> What vice has it subdu'd? Whose heart reclaim'd
> By rigour, or whom laugh'd into reform?
> Alas! Leviathan is not so tam'd.

Even Voltaire (who had himself been victimized by libellers) harshly condemned his favorite mode in arguments drawn from Bayle: "If I followed my taste, I would speak of satire only in order to inspire abhorrence and to arm virtue against this dangerous form of writing. Satire is almost always unjust, and that is its least defect. . . . It is a trade, like selling adulterated wine. One must admit that there is hardly a trade more unworthy, more cowardly, and more punishable."

By the early nineteenth century the word *satire* had acquired in the popular mind a wide range of generally unpleasant associations. Lady Middleton, in Jane Austen's *Sense and Sensibility* (1811), dislikes Elinor and Marianne Dashwood: ". . . because they were fond of reading, she fancied them satirical: perhaps without exactly knowing what it was to be satirical; but *that* did not signify. It was censure in common use, and easily given." Thackeray's defense of satire in mid-century is totally revealing. He has been deploring the savagery of the caricaturists Gilray and [Thomas] Rowlandson: "We cannot afford to lose Satyr with his pipe and dances and gambols. But we have washed, combed, clothed, and taught the rogue good manners: or rather, let us say, he has learned them himself; for he is of nature soft and kindly, and he has put aside his mad pranks and tipsy habits; and frolicsome always, has become gentle and harmless, smitten into shame by the pure presence of our women and the sweet confiding smiles of our children." Shame, the instrument by which the satirist once killed, and later purported to bring about moral reform, has, in this view, tamed the satirist himself—perhaps a final variation on the satirist-satirized theme. The fear and the hatred have disappeared: but so, clearly, has the satire.

THE RELATION BETWEEN SATIRE AND SOCIETY

The whole theme of the satirist's ambiguous relation to society is neatly encapsulated, I think, at the end of Juvenal's first satire. The full-blown description of Rome's insanely abandoned ways comes to a climax as Juvenal considers the situation of the poet. No time has ever needed him more, he proclaims: all vice is at its acme, and Juvenal exhorts the poet to spread his sails, to shake out every stitch of canvas. But then the recollection of danger intervenes. Where is the freedom our heroic forefathers had to attack the wicked, to name the evildoer? Anyone who today dared describe Nero's master in debauchery, Tigellinus, would be burned at the stake in the arena. It was not always so: ". . . when Lucilius roars and rages as if with sword in hand, the hearer, whose soul is cold with crime, grows red; he sweats with the secret consciousness of sin. Hence wrath and tears." The image of the satirist projected here is that of a hero; but, "inde ira et lacrimae" ["Hence wrath and tears"]—he is a hated hero. The wrath is that of the victim for the satirist; as the context indicates, he may be capable of doing the poet great harm. But the victim also turns red and sweats in his consciousness of guilt. The tears are his as well as the anger. The satire, heroically issued, has aroused wrath and fear; yet it has also performed its moral function. In the phrase "inde ira et lacrimae" is epitomized the purported function of satire and, by implication, the ambiguous situation of the satirist in relation to his contemporaries.

Society has many grounds for its dislike and distrust of satire. No matter what abuses it may expose, no matter what lofty motives the satirist may profess, he has no *right* (so goes the chief moral argument) to take the honor and reputation of other men into his hands or to set himself up as a censor of established institutions or modes of behavior. Further, for all the pain he causes, the satirist never actually brings about reform. These are the objections most often stated. But society has other reasons for dubiety. The pressure of the satirist's art inevitably comes athwart society's efforts to maintain its equilibrium. The satirist usually claims that he does not attack institutions; he attacks perversions of institutions. When, for example, he ridicules a corrupt judge he intends no reflection on the law as such; he is attacking a corruption which has crept into the law. Ben Jonson's Cordatus, the "Moderator" of *Every Man Out of his Humour*, speaks precisely to this point. The innocent will not be injured in this play, he says; to claim injury would be "to affirme, that a man, writing of NERO, should meane all Emperors: or speaking of MACHIAVEL, comprehend all States-men; or in our SORDIDO, all Farmars; and so of the rest: then which, nothing can be utter'd more malicious, or absurd." In large measure, of course, Cordatus is right. As Northrop Frye says, the satirist attacks primarily neither the man nor the institution; he attacks an evil man who is given gigantic stature and protected by the prestige of the institution. "The cowl might make the monk if it were not for the satirist."

But there is another sense in which Cordatus is wrong, for an attack by a powerful satirist on a local phenomenon seems to be capable of indefinite extension in the reader's mind into an attack on the whole structure of which that phenomenon is part. Significantly, I think, this imaginative process is magical; it functions by synecdoche, which is one of the foundations of magic. In "mythico-linguistic thought," to use Cassirer's phrase, the part does not merely represent the whole, it *is* the whole; by the magical process of identification the nail paring or the lock of hair from an enemy *is* the enemy, and whoever controls the part has dominion also over the whole. This process is by no means confined to a mythically bound society; as a different order of experience, to be sure, it is the way of the imagination when it is bound, in its own way, by the spell of the creative artist. The judge who has been ridiculed by a powerful satirist comes to stand for—to be—lawyers in general and even the law itself. What starts as local attack ends by calling the whole institution into question. Thus the satirical portraits of [Geoffrey] Chaucer, who seems to have been thoroughly orthodox in religion, have often been interpreted as evidence of his revolt against the Church; during the Reformation he and [William] Langland were used for purposes doubtless far removed from their intent. Molière proposed in *Tartuffe* to unmask an example of religious hypocrisy. Yet the effect of the play has seemed to many people genuinely subversive, the attack on the hypocrite somehow, insidiously, becoming an attack on religion itself. Two hundred and fifty years after the play was first performed, Brunetière could write that the wound had not closed: ". . . there is no doubt that it was deep; that the hand which made it meant to make it; that therefore it was not only false devotion but also true, which Molière meant to attack. . . ." Brunetière attributes the damage to Molière's evil intentions; in an odd way, if one wants to talk about damage, one is on safer grounds to speak of magic: of synecdoche, of the tainted part becoming through the strange efficacies of art the whole.

RELIGIOUS AND PHILOSOPHICAL SATIRES

The *Tartuffe* dilemma is very ancient; Lucian's dialogue *The Dead Come to Life* turns precisely on it. The question of the dialogue is this: has Lucian's ridicule of individual philosophers (specifically in *Philosophies for Sale*) besmirched Phi-

losophy herself? The problem is treated with the greatest
subtlety. Frankness (a transparent alias for Lucian) is hailed
up for trial; he is to be accused by Socrates, Plato, Diogenes,
and others who are on leave from Hades for a day, and is to
be judged by Philosophy. In the course of the trial the following points are established: Philosophy holds that ridicule, far
from harming truth, actually enhances it; Lucian is found to
have ridiculed, not Philosophy, but only impostors and thus
to have served truth; and the character of the satirist is established to be that of a "bluff-hater, cheat-hater, liar-hater,
vanity-hater," but also that of a "truth-lover, beauty-lover,
simplicity-lover," and so on. These latter propensities the
satirist has little opportunity to exercise, the world being
what it is; but Philosophy consoles him: "the two callings
[hating evil and loving good] . . . are but one." Philosophy expresses in a phrase the public rationale of the satirist's activity. Lucian manages his own defense with marvellous skill
and impeccable logic; the fact remains, however, that as all
readers of Lucian know, Philosophy emerges from his dialogues in very tattered condition indeed.

Swift notoriously found himself in a similar situation with
A Tale of a Tub. In the "Apology" which he added to the work
in 1710, he reverts at least six times to the contention that the
Tale attacks, not religion and learning, but abuses in religion
and learning: *"Religion they tell us ought not to be ridiculed,
and they tell us Truth, yet surely the Corruptions in it may; for
we are taught by the tritest Maxim in the World, that Religion
being the best of Things, its Corruptions are likely to be the
worst."* Yet the attack, as Swift's contemporaries saw, could
hardly be contained; restricted as the intention may have
been, the *Tale* in effect ramified into an attack on religion itself. I believe that Swift was deeply concerned for the welfare
of the Established Church as he saw it; but under the impact
of his satire one of the great pillars of society rocked a bit.
Swift's strength, as Empson puts it, made his instrument too
strong for him. His magic, one might say, was his undoing.

The implications are reasonably clear. The satirist, it is
true, claims to be conservative, to be using his art to shore
up the foundations of the established order; and insofar as
one can place satirists politically, I suspect that a large majority are what would be called conservative. Professor
Auerbach has emphasized, for example, that in all Molière's
plays there is no criticism whatever of the social, political, or

economic bases of life. "Molière's criticism is entirely moral-istic; that is to say; it accepts the prevailing structure of soci-ety, takes for granted its justification, permanence, and gen-eral validity, and castigates the excesses occurring within its limits as ridiculous." Yet who could deny the profoundly an-archic thrust of Alceste's sentiments? The play [*The Misan-thrope*] demands that his passionate utterances be given full weight in the scale which measures his fanatical sincerity against the social hypocrisy of the Orontes, the Célimènes, the Philintes of his world. It demands that he be taken seri-ously; and the demand enforces the question: what if he *were* taken seriously? Alceste's commitments and criticisms are moral, as Auerbach says, rather than social or political; but in the area of his interest, and given the power of his ut-terance, the moral subsumes the social. His ideas are radi-cally disruptive. It is hard to conceive the society that could sustain them.

THE REVOLUTIONARY ASPECT OF SATIRE

Such ambiguous results seem almost an inevitable conse-quence of major satire. Let the conscious intent of the artist be what it will, the local attack cannot be contained: the ironic language eats its way in implication through the most powerful-seeming structures. One final example from Swift. The complexly simple projector of *An Argument against Abolishing Christianity,* the "I" of the piece, argues cogently for the retention of nominal Christianity. To restore "real" Christianity, he says, "would indeed be a wild Project; it would be to dig up Foundations; . . . to break the entire Frame and Constitution of Things; to ruin Trade, extinguish Arts and Sciences, with the Professors of them; in short, to turn our Courts, Exchanges, and Shops into Desarts. . . ." One reads this and one can only say, He is right: the fool speaks truth. Between Swift and the projector, of course, there is a considerable ironic remove, just as there is distance between Swift and some of the meanings set in motion by his creature. We may doubt that Swift the Tory politician, Swift the social man, would have sympathized with breaking the "Frame and Constitution of Things." But here Swift is the artist. The pres-sure of his art works directly against the ostensibly conser-vative function which it is said to serve. Instead of shoring up foundations, it tears them down. It is revolutionary.

Society has doubtless been wise, in its old pragmatic way,

to suspect the satirist. Whether he is an enchanter wielding the ambiguous power of magic, or whether he is a "mere" poet, his relation to society will necessarily be problematic. He is of society in the sense that his art must be grounded in his experience as social man; but he must also be apart, as he struggles to achieve aesthetic distance. His practice is often sanative, as he proclaims; but it may be revolutionary in ways that society cannot possibly approve, and in ways that may not be clear even to the satirist.

The Future of Satire

Matthew Hodgart

In the following selection, Matthew Hodgart evaluates the future of satire as a genre of literature and as an art form in general. He concludes that while literary satire may never return to its earlier heights, it continues to thrive in cinema and cartoons. Hodgart asserts that film is especially successful at communicating satire because it can achieve the correct balance between realism and fantasy, as seen in the works of Charlie Chaplin and Georg Wilhelm Pabst. Likewise, cartoons can be an especially powerful form of satire due to their wide audience appeal. However, literary satire faces several obstacles if it is to regain prominence, in particular a world that seeks compromise and is not as welcoming of the rigid views common to satire. Hodgart was a professor of English at the University of Sussex in England and the author of several books, including biographies of Samuel Johnson and James Joyce and *Satire*, the source of the following selection.

Satire does not end with the novel or with . . . other forms of literature. . . . It is not even confined to 'polite letters', that is, to the more conventional and dignified forms of literature. Excellent satire has always been found in journalism throughout the history of the periodical press; and journalism includes not only the newspaper and magazine but the popular song: as we have seen, the broadside ballad was once a most effective vehicle. This is to be expected: the political satirist in particular must try to reach a wide public if he is to achieve his ends, and any popular medium will serve his purpose. It would have been interesting, if there had been space, to follow the development of satire in modern journalism, from the reviews of pre-Hitler Germany, through the famous French weekly *Le Canard Enchaîné* to

Excerpted from *Satire* by Matthew Hodgart (New York: McGraw-Hill, 1969). Copyright 1969 by Matthew Hodgart.

London's *Private Eye*. . . . There has often been a close link between the satiric little magazines, the entertainers of cabaret and revue, and the cartoonists, as is the case with *Private Eye;* and it is likely that satire will continue to flourish in such mixed and complementary forms. The most fruitful extension of such kinds of informal satire has come about by means of the gramophone record and sound-tape, which can catch the spontaneous impromptu performance of the entertainer, and best of all by means of television. This medium, which is not yet satisfactory for formal drama, is highly suited to the intimacy and informality of the *chansonnier*[1] style, to improvised miming and to the loose structure of the revue. Documentary illustrations and the art of the cartoonist, still or animated, can be interwoven with satirical songs, sketches and monologues. This mixture was first used successfully in Britain in the satirical programme *That Was The Week That Was,* which with David Frost as *compère* had great success in 1962–3 and has had several less entertaining sequels. This kind of programme presupposes a public that is fairly sophisticated about politics, as the British public of the sixties seems to have become, after a decade of education by television; and in turn it perhaps heightens the political awareness of the public.

SATIRE IN CINEMA AND CARTOONS

Whether television can foster great satirical art is doubtful—that the cinema can is certain. The cinema has been used successfully to translate some of the classics of literary satire into a universal visual language, and it has produced satirical classics of its own. The medium offers many advantages for satire: in particular, the possibility of achieving the proper balance between fantasy and realism, which seems to be essential for the communication of a satiric message. The main disadvantage of the cinema is that it is vulnerable to censorship and, even more than television, to commercial pressure: a moving picture is a very expensive undertaking, and the sponsors may want to avoid taking risks with outspoken criticism. Satirical pictures about life in Russia during the Stalin era were forbidden and have been slow to emerge in recent years. An adaptation of [Pierre Choderlos

1. Chansonniers are people who perform or write chansons, which are French cabaret or classical songs. Among the popular chanson styles are satirical cabaret songs.

de] Laclos' great satiric novel *Les Liaisons Dangereuses* was for a while refused an export licence by the French government on the grounds that it presented an unflattering and allegedly distorted image of modern French life. The brilliantly funny film about unofficial strikes *I'm all right, Jack* (Boulting Brothers 1959, with Peter Sellers) is said to have been made under protest from certain trade unions. Hence good satirical films have usually been made in fairly free political conditions or by independent producers with modest financial backing.

The classic of adaptation is [Georg Wilhelm] Pabst's *Dreigroschenoper* (*The Threepenny Opera*, 1931), a free reworking of the musical play by Brecht and Kurt Weill. Some of the verbal wit and intellectual complexity of the original are lost, but the combination of elegant stylisation and low-life realism is beautifully realised. The anarchistic spirit of Brecht (and of John Gay and Villon, who inspired Brecht) comes across with great force, as does Pabst's addition of the final all-conquering march of the beggars.

The first and greatest name in original film satire is Charlie Chaplin. He has created the most moving and enduring image of the century—the little man lost in the alien world or the city jungle, surviving only by his ingenuity and stoic cheerfulness. *Modern Times* (1936) is his first full-length satire, on the theme of machine technology and mass production and their effect on the individual. The memorable opening uses a basic device of satire: sheep go down a gangway, cut to workers entering a factory. The machines take control: Charlie is fed by one and, driven mad by the assembly line, he turns into a machine. These despairingly funny scenes make a noble protest against dehumanisation. *The Great Dictator* (1940, but begun before the war in 1939) is courageous political satire, a marvellous burlesque of Hitler and a protest against the brutalities of his régime at a time when many Europeans and Americans were willing to tolerate Nazism. It could not have been made any later, since Hitler in the 1940s was no longer a subject for satire; but at the right moment Chaplin spoke for the world's conscience and made the world laugh. Despite the failure of his later films, Chaplin earned a place of honour in the history of political satire. There are not many other classics in this field. In Germany the tradition of Pabst was taken up again in *Wir Wunderkinder* (*Aren't We Wonderful:* Kurt Hoffmann, Western Germany, 1958), describing the parallel lives of two schoolboy friends, one a Nazi, from the First World War to the 'economic miracle'; there are interludes in the action with songs in the style of the pre-war Berlin satirical revues, and this stylisation allows the subject of chicanery and graft to be presented with witty detachment.

There are many examples of 'sub-satire' in the cinema, including Hollywood comedies that offer ironic exposures of social abuses, the charming fantasies of René Clair (especially *À Nous la Liberté*, 1931) and of Jacques Tati, and the surrealistic violence of Luis Bunuel. Finally one should mention the achievements and potential of the animated cartoon: [George] Orwell's *Animal Farm* has been the basis for a cartoon film, and the imaginative possibilities of the form have been shown by Dick Williams in *The Little Island*, 1955.

Here we return to traditional visual satire, that is, to caricature and cartoon. I have not attempted to trace the origin and history of this art: the illustrations must tell their own story. Cartoon means a fantastic composition, often some kind of allegory and usually on a political topic; caricature is the distorted portraiture of individuals. In combination since the eighteenth century, they have probably been the most popular and influential form of satire. This is the most literary kind of visual art, intimately connected with journalism. Most literate people in the world turn every day, or at least week, to their favourite cartoonist for his comment on current affairs. But even before the mass circulation of newspapers began, cartoons could reach a very large section of the public through the medium of woodcuts, engravings and lithographs. Like literary satire, the art of the cartoonist is essentially ephemeral but occasionally, as with [William] Hogarth, [James] Gillray, [Honoré] Goya or [Francisco] Daumier, may ascend to greatness. Again, as in literature, the dividing line between propaganda and imaginative creation is difficult to define, but in both there must be a dimension of fantasy and travesty, and a spirit of free criticism. The art of caricature and cartoon is obviously still thriving, and in free societies its future seems as assured as any human institution can be.

An Uncertain Future

It is not clear, however, that we can have the same confidence in the future of literary satire. In this survey [his book,

Satire] I have not taken the history of literature up to the present day (apart from mentioning a few examples in poetry,
drama and the novel); if I had done so, I should have been
hard put to it to find many great satirists still alive and producing. But this is also true of other kinds of literature: there
is currently also a shortage of first-class poets and novelists.
We have passed through a great age, which reached its peak
about 1910 to 1940, the age of [William Butler] Yeats, [Rainer
Maria] Rilke, [James] Joyce, [Franz] Kafka, [Thomas] Mann
and [Marcel] Proust; and the contemporary scene in Europe
is one of imaginative exhaustion and the exploitation of minor talents. Since this kind of trough has appeared many
times before in history, it would be absurd to speak of the
present or future death of literature. The printed word, in the
service of art and the human spirit, is potent and will revive.
But will satire also revive? As journalistic comment on the
absurdities of politics and manners it has never been in danger of dying out except when political freedom has been in
danger, and in the open society it should have as permanent
a future as caricature and cartoon. But that satire will again
cross the frontier into the enchanted realm of imaginative
literature, as it has done many times in the past, is difficult
to predict. It may be that the modern world makes too great
demands on the writers; demands, that is, for understanding
the ever more rapidly increasing changes caused by science
and technology, and for flexibility in dealing with these
changes. The satirist, after all, traditionally takes up a rigid
stance in the face of change; he does not want to understand
everything. He is committed to militant action, while the
modern world increasingly asks for peace, negotiation and
the often tedious examination of problems. Just as hot war
has become too expensive a luxury for mankind, so the war
of words may become too great an expenditure of effort for
the writer. Again, the world is becoming de-ritualised.
Throughout history men have defended themselves against
a hostile universe, not just by their practical efficiency, but
by the ritual forms they invent and preserve, in religion, politics and social life, forms of ceremony, dress and rhetoric.
The satirists, as l have tried to show, have always attacked
these rituals whenever they have found them absurd; and
they have often invented mock rituals, parodies and traves-
ties of ceremony, like mock-heroic poetry, to enshrine folly
and vice. But ritual behaviour is now felt to be less and less

appropriate to the conditions of our life; we are being forced into informality, whether of dress, manners or speech: in political debate and literature traditional rhetoric is going out of favour. So the satirist is becoming deprived of many of his favourite targets, and his readers may fail to enjoy or understand his elaborate rituals of parody.

The satirist, however, has always accepted the risk of failure: by committing himself to the exposure of public abuses, he allows himself to be caught up in the ephemeral and transitory events of his day. When these events have receded into the night of history—as many of the topics mentioned in these pages have done—his work may be overtaken by oblivion, or at best live on only for the antiquarian. The greatest satire not only fixes a moment of history in a frozen attitude of absurdity, and makes the event a permanent and ludicrous warning to the future, but it tells the truth about the depths of human nature, which do not change. Satire warns us that man is a dangerous animal, with an infinite capacity for folly; and when it has said that well, it has said enough. It is for the poets to speak of man's glory.

Satire Is No Longer Relevant

Lewis H. Lapham

In August 1996, Dick Morris—an adviser to President
Clinton—resigned when his affair with a prostitute,
with whom he had shared political secrets, became
public. In the following essays, Lewis H. Lapham,
the editor of *Harper's Magazine*, uses the Morris
scandal and the 1996 Democratic and Republican
presidential conventions to argue that satire is no
longer a relevant form of literature in America.
Lapham contends that although the political scene in
1996 was ripe for satire, the overall media reaction
lacked all but the mildest irony. He also asserts that
America in the late twentieth century has generally
been uncomfortable with satire and dissent, prefer-
ring conformity and entertainment that depicts the
lives of most fortunate members of society. In addition to editing *Harper's*, Lapham is an author who
has published several collections of essays and
whose work has appeared in numerous publications,
including *Vanity Fair* and the *New York Times*.

> *Well, humor is the great thing, the saving thing, after all.*
> —Mark Twain.

On the same afternoon in early September [1996] that Ran-
dom House offered Dick Morris $2.5 million for yet another
book applying yet another coat of mud to the character of
President Bill Clinton, I ran across three New York editors in
the lobby bar of the Algonquin Hotel who read in the an-
nouncement yet another reason to mourn the passing of H.L.
Mencken. Sitting under the potted palms familiar in the
1930s to the Algonquin roundtable of celebrated wits
(among them Harpo Marx and Dorothy Parker), and being

literary people old enough to remember the world before television, they buttressed their remarks with invidious comparisons between time past and time present. Here was the braggart Morris, a rank opportunist newly famous for his adoration of a prostitute's toes, but where was the writer capable of skewering the fellow on the spit of satire? Where was Mencken? Where, for that matter, were Ambrose Bierce and Mark Twain? What had become of "our native genius for brutal sarcasm and savage wit"? The earth groaned under the weight of scoundrels and fools, but deliverance was nowhere at hand, or even in sight.

MODERN RECEPTION OF MENCKEN

The three editors pursued the subject for the better part of an hour, ordering more gin and adding names to their list of books and authors deserving of death by ridicule, and by the time the waiter brought the third round of drinks, I was imagining Mencken miraculously risen from the grave, pushing through the doors of the hotel with a cigar in his mouth and a manuscript under his arm. Like Bierce and Twain, the sage of Baltimore was not known for his deference to the pieties of the age, and I thought it probable that within a matter of a very few minutes, the two ladies and one gentleman regretting his absence would find even more pressing reasons to regret his presence. Some of Mencken's offhand remarks came more or less readily to mind—his classification of Franklin D. Roosevelt as a demagogue of the same ilk as Mussolini, his description of Philadelphia as "an intellectual slum," his belief that even an absolute and intransigent monarchy was "appreciably superior" to the American system of democratic government, his contempt for the average man, his definition of the American politician, any American politician, as a man who crawls and "knows the taste of the boot-polish." Except for the last remark (permissible only if pertaining to Morris or a dead Nazi), few or none of Mencken's opinions would make themselves welcome on the editorial page of the newspaper that the woman on my right served as a leading liberal ornament, or on the fall list of the publishing house that the gentleman on my left devoted to the manufacture of celebrity biographies, all or most of which could carry the uniform title *My Life on the B-List* or *All About Me.*

Off the record and among themselves, the editors in distress were free to despise the manuscripts they ushered into the light of print, even to mock the generally accepted notions of government and law, but in their public personae as protectors of the nation's intellectual health and moral safety, they could no more afford to publish Mencken than they could afford to question the beauty of Maya Angelou's poems or fail to give thanks for the benefactions of Cardinal O'Connor and Rupert Murdoch.

A DISSENT-FREE SOCIETY

Their predicament prompted me to wonder about the uses of satire in a society that appears to have lost its appetite for objection and dissent. Like Mencken, Twain thought of humor, especially in its more violent forms of invective and burlesque, as a weapon with which to attack pride victorious and evil arrogant. He placed the ferocity of his wit at the service of his conscience, pitting it against the "peacock shams" of the established order. Harboring no goodwill for what he called the "colossal humbug" of the world, he believed that "only laughter can blow it away at a blast."

The laughter that both Twain and Mencken had in mind has been remanded to smaller magazines and the comedy clubs very far from Broadway. The marketing directors who make the rules of commercial publishing regard humor of any kind as so specialized a commodity that the chain bookstores make no distinction between the works of Voltaire and those of Garfield the cat; both authors appear under signs marked HUMOR in order that the prospective reader will be advised to approach them with caution. The words might not mean exactly what they say.

In the respectable newspapers most of the commentary about Morris's sexual behavior was as literal-minded as *The Celestine Prophecy* or a book about how to make a fortune in Florida real estate. Several columnists remembered that it was Morris who had cajoled President Clinton into espousing the cause of family values, but their ironies were mild and offered little proof of the "native genius for brutal sarcasm and savage wit." A number of other columnists submitted statements on behalf of women's rights and the sacrament of marriage, but nothing much was said about Morris turning his term of White House service into a handsomely illustrated slander of the

President. The practice has become standard over the last thirty years and no longer invites scorn. The media were more impressed by Morris's appearance on two successive covers of *Time* magazine, which moved them to jealous speculations about his enhanced worth on the talk-show and lecture circuits.

Nor did the general run of discussion about the season's presidential campaign amount to much more than a querulous complaint about the tawdriness of the rhetoric and the lack of noble sentiment. Ted Koppel removed the *Nightline* cameras from the Republican Convention in San Diego because the proceedings failed to meet his standard of portentousness, and except for Russell Baker in the *New York Times*, the upscale columnists in the respectable newspapers, eschewing satire for the safer course of indignant viewing-with-alarm, managed to sound like upscale food and furniture critics forced to shop at a Walmart in Brockton, Massachusetts. Instead of being offered antique oratory as finely worked as a Tiffany lamp (memorable phrases, eloquent debates in old wooden rotundas, the voice of William Jennings Bryan), they were being presented with freeze-dried sound bites meant to be dropped into boiling water on *Larry King Live*.

The criticisms seemed a trifle churlish and unfair. Both candidates were doing their patriotic best to supply the desired atmospheres of a lost golden age—Hillary Clinton evoking the memory of a nineteenth-century American village green; her husband waving from a train that once had carried Harry Truman east from St. Louis; Jack Kemp permitting himself the wistful hope for a triumphant return to the gold standard; candidate [Senator Bob] Dole saying in his acceptance speech that "all things flow from doing what is right . . . only right conduct distinguishe[s] a great nation from one that cannot rise above itself. It has never been otherwise . . ." But the media, like Queen Victoria, were not amused.

Mencken, on the other hand, would have vastly enjoyed the proud display of hypocrisies. I could imagine him rummaging through the histories of ancient Rome, the Renaissance papacy, and imperial Spain in a comically fruitless search for proofs of the theorem that great nations achieve their places in the world by doing what is right. And when he had done with the chaste and righteous acts performed by such exemplars of Christian deportment as Cesare Borgia and Cardinal Richelieu and Otto von Bismarck,[1] I could imagine him coming at last to the bathos of Vice President Al Gore and the weeping for Christopher Reeve, mocking the rose-colored images of the American paradise shaped by the milk-white hand of Providence, the citadel of virtue and ark of innocence, a nation so favored by God and Pat Robertson that it never killed a buffalo or a Cherokee Indian, never ran a gambling casino or lynched a Negro or bribed a judge or elected a president as stupid as Warren Harding. And because it had behaved itself so well (always doing right, always dressed for church), it had become a land entirely overgrown with honeysuckle, where the urban poor go quietly off to reservations in Utah and nobody, not even Dick Morris, fornicates on Sunday afternoons.

WHY AMERICA DISLIKES SATIRE

The satirist attempts the crime of arson, meaning to set a torch of words (what Twain called "painted fire") to the hospitality tents of pompous and self-righteous cant. The intention presupposes readers well enough aware of their own hypocrisies to see the stone of truth hidden behind the back of the easy and not so genial smile. The country has never produced such readers in commercial quantity. Even if Mencken or Twain were to receive the necessary permission from the editors in the Algonquin bar, where is the audience likely to be heartened by the news that a society based on cash and self-interest is not a society at all but a state of war? Notwithstanding the slides shown at the political conventions in San Diego and Chicago (the ones about the nonviolent and peace-loving people at play in the fields of the Lord), America is a country in which the Goodyear blimp often returns from its pleasant afternoon over the golf course riddled with bullet holes, a country in which 135,000 children bring guns to school, where a doctor is more likely to be punished for overcharging a patient than for killing or maiming one, where the labor conditions in the California

1. Cesare Borgia was the illegitimate son of Rodrigo Borgia, who later became Pope Alexander VI. A year after his father was elected to the papacy, Cesare was made a cardinal. He was known for his bad habits and violent temper and was believed to have been involved in the assassination of his brother Giovanni. Cardinal Richelieu was a cardinal and statesman who in 1624 became King Louis XIII's chief minister. His policies helped bring absolutism to France. Otto von Bismarck helped transform Germany from a loose collection of states into a unified empire. He served as the unified nation's first chancellor, from 1871–1890.

strawberry fields are as destructive of human health and
well-being as the explosion on TWA Flight 800, only over a
slightly longer period of time, where a gang of thieves in
Brooklyn robs banks with a backhoe, and where, with the
hair shorn from the head and beard of Ted Kaczynski, a
Montana barber ties trout flies called "The Bomber." Satire
is humor sent on a moral errand, but the book-buying public is more familiar with publicity tours.

As forms of literary address, we nearly always have preferred the sermon and the sales pitch, and we seldom have
had much use or liking for the voices of dissent. Tom Paine
made the mistake of extending his defense of human liberty
into a philippic against the despotism of the Christian
Church, an impiety for which he was reviled as a heretic,
scorned as a drunkard, and denied church burial in the
country that he had done so much to set free from England.
American society turned out to be profoundly conformist,
suspicious of any idea that couldn't be yoked to the wheel of
progress, deeply reverent in the presence of wealth. Wit was
predictably disastrous, and the ambitious clerk or college
man soon learned that in the troubled sea of worldly affairs
one sinks by levity and rises by gravity. Success entailed the

A DISADVANTAGE OF SATIRE

In the following excerpt from his book, Introduction to
Satire, *Leonard Feinberg suggests that one of the reasons
satire is unpopular is because it is often written about unpleasant subjects, while the average reader prefers literature that com-
forts. Feinberg is a professor emeritus of English at Iowa State.*

Satire bears a bad name. Even writers interested in it have
made disparaging remarks about it. [George] Meredith's famous essay distinguished sharply between humor, which he
admired, and satire, which he called venomous and disrep-
utable. The author of the only history of English satire, Hugh
Walker, concluded that "satire at its best is a second-rate type
of literature." And Joseph Conrad dismissed satire as an inad-
equate art form. . . .

[One] disadvantage of satire is that s*ome truths are simply
too uncomfortable to admit,* or to live with for more than a
brief period at a time. The best-selling books are sentimental
or historical or religious or sex-filled novels; the public knows
what it wants. It is true that much of this popular literature

keeping up of sober appearances and never venturing an opinion likely to affront the Mr. Pecksniff who owned the feed store. By the end of the nineteenth century satire had been largely confined to its gentler expressions (the kind that didn't need to be kept out of the hands of children), and Twain was obliged to reserve his more acerbic observations for posthumous publication, in the meantime playing the part of the harmless clown. Edith Wharton left for Europe, Finley Peter Dunne put on the mask of Mr. Dooley, and Bierce walked off the set into the deserts of northern Mexico.

THE DECAY OF AMERICAN SATIRE

Briefly revived during the intermission between World Wars I and II, the satirical spirit showed to brilliant effect not only among the Algonquin wits but also in the writings of Don Marquis, James Thurber, Albert J. Nock, Dawn Powell, and Sinclair Lewis, but the moment didn't last. Following upon its victories in the Second World War, the United States found itself transformed into an imperial power, and the delusions of grandeur had their usual ill effect. The fear of nuclear annihilation inhibited any sudden or subversive movement of the literary imagination, and the glorious return to economic

also contains unpleasant material. But unlike popular literature and tragedy, both of which provide a natural emotional relief—tears—satire offers only the "unnatural" (socially conditioned) relief of laughter.

But life is not that funny, and satire remains an artificial technique for adapting to existence. Though Dr. Edmund Bergler overstates his case as usual when he says that men joke not because they are in a gay mood but only because they are "furnishing inner defenses in reply to a monster, conscience," nevertheless it is true that significant satire offers much more than gaiety. Satire that survives is likely to deal with serious subjects and to emphasize the unpleasant aspects of those subjects. Most readers do not like to be exposed to unpleasantness—or, if they are, they want to be comforted and reassured about the unpleasantness. Satire, far from comforting or reassuring, exaggerates the disagreeable elements to a distressing degree, as in Mencken's remark: "The meek shall inherit the earth—and the strong will take it away from them."

Leonard Feinberg, *Introduction to Satire.* Ames: Iowa State University Press, 1967.

prosperity restored the statues of Mammon to their golden pedestals in the country's better department stores. The country's governing and possessing classes, admiring their new patents of omnipotence in the mirror of an increasingly jingoistic press, acquired the habit of taking themselves very, very seriously indeed. They didn't look with favor upon the kind of jokes that cast doubt on the guarantees of immortality and the promise of redemption, and within the remarkably short space of the same six or seven years that brought forth the McCarthy hearings,[2] the decay of the American satirical spirit begins to show up in the pages of the national magazines, the change of tone as clearly marked as the edges of the Gulf Stream when seen from a height of 20,000 feet. Prior to 1955, the writing exhibits the characteristics of people willing to laugh at their own vanity and intolerance; after 1955 the writing turns heavy and solemn, the authors laboring under the weight of sententious political theory and gazing into the wells of Narcissus.

If before 1960 it was possible to define literature, politics, journalism, and the movies as separate provinces of expression, over the last forty-odd years they have been fused into the alloy of the entertainment media and made subjects of an empire ruled by television. The television audience prefers situation comedy to satire, situation comedy and maybe the kind of sarcasm (pointed, but not so pointed as to lose the market) that lends itself to gridiron dinners, Academy Awards ceremonies, and *Saturday Night Live.* And because the television audience wishes to include itself in the good life seen on the screen (traveling to Europe, choosing between the Mercedes and the Lexus, conversing with Heather Locklear), the class bias of American humor, which once favored the least fortunate members of society at the expense of their self-important overlords, reversed direction, and much of what now passes for merry witticism on *Seinfeld* or *The Late Show with David Letterman* (as well as in the writing of P.J. O'Rourke or Rush Limbaugh) plays on the anxi-

2. In April 1954, Joseph McCarthy, a senator from Wisconsin who had garnered national attention for his allegations of Communist infiltration of the U.S. government, accused Secretary of the Army Robert T. Stevens and his aides of attempting to hide evidence of espionage. In response, the army accused McCarthy and two aides of improperly seeking preferential treatment for an army private who had been a former consultant to the Senate subcommittee on investigations, which McCarthy chaired. Following highly publicized hearings, McCarthy and his aides were cleared of the charges that August. However, his fellow senators condemned McCarthy in December 1954 for his contempt and abusive behavior toward a Senate elections subcommittee that had investigated the senator in 1952, various senators, and the Senate as a whole.

eties endured by the most fortunate members of the society when confronted with apparitions from the lower depths— scary street persons, hostile waitresses, ugly dogs. Given the trend of the times, it is conceivable that Morris could show up on *Oprah*, wearing his cute sailor hat, presenting himself as a victim unjustly exploited by the yellow press, saying that not all prostitutes these days have hearts of gold.

I mentioned the possibility to the editorial committee assembled in the Algonquin bar, but they interpreted the suggestion as a marketing strategy instead of a sarcasm, and I knew that Mencken wasn't coming back to West Forty-fourth Street and that when Twain said that satire preserved men from being "shrivelled into sheep," it didn't occur to him that lamb's wool would come to be so much admired.

CHRONOLOGY

CA. 448

Aristophanes is born.

423

Aristophanes writes *The Clouds.*

422

Aristophanes writes *The Wasps.*

414

Aristophanes writes *The Birds.*

411

Aristophanes writes *Lysistrata* and *Thesmorphoriazusae.*

405

Aristophanes writes *The Frogs.*

393

Aristophanes writes *Ecclesiazusa.*

385

Aristophanes dies.

65

Horace is born.

35

Horace writes the first book of *Satires.*

30

Horace writes the second book of *Satires.*

23

Horace writes *Odes.*

8

Horace dies.

A.D.

CA. 65
Juvenal is born.

98–128
Juvenal writes *The Sixteen Satires.*

CA. 128
Juvenal dies.

CA. 1343
Geoffrey Chaucer is born.

1387–1400
Chaucer writes *The Canterbury Tales.*

1400
Chaucer dies.

1494
François Rabelais is born.

1532
Rabelais writes *Pantagruel.*

1534
Rabelais publishes *Gargantua.*

1547
Miguel de Cervantes Saavedra is born.

1553
Rabelais dies.

1572
Ben Jonson is born.

1601
Jonson writes *The Poetaster.*

1605
Cervantes publishes Part 1 of *Don Quixote.*

1606
Jonson writes *Volpone.*

1614
Jonson writes *Bartholomew Fair.*

1615

Cervantes publishes Part 2 of *Don Quixote.*

1616

Cervantes dies.

1637

Jonson dies.

1667

Jonathan Swift is born.

1688

Alexander Pope is born.

1694

Voltaire (François Marie Arouet) is born.

1697

Swift publishes *The Battle of the Books.*

1704

Swift publishes *A Tale of a Tub.*

1712

Pope publishes "The Rape of the Lock."

1726

Swift publishes *Gulliver's Travels.*

1728

Pope publishes *Dunciad.*

1729

Swift publishes "A Modest Proposal."

1744

Pope dies.

1745

Swift dies.

1759

Voltaire publishes *Candide.*

1775

Jane Austen is born.

1778

Voltaire dies.

1788

Lord Byron (George Gordon Byron) is born.

1809

Byron publishes *English Bards and Scotch Reviewers.*

1813

Austen publishes *Pride and Prejudice.*

1817

Austen dies.

1818

Austen's *Northanger Abbey* is posthumously published.

1818–1819

Byron writes Cantos I and II of *Don Juan.*

1823

Don Juan is completed.

1824

Byron dies.

1835

Mark Twain (Samuel Langhorne Clemens) is born.

1869

Twain publishes *Innocents Abroad.*

1884

Twain publishes *Adventures of Huckleberry Finn.*

1885

Sinclair Lewis is born.

1889

Twain publishes *A Connecticut Yankee in King Arthur's Court.*

1894

Aldous Huxley is born.

1903

George Orwell (Eric Arthur Blair) is born.

1910

Twain dies.

1920

Lewis publishes *Main Street*.

1922

Lewis publishes *Babbitt*; Kurt Vonnegut Jr. is born.

1923

Joseph Heller is born.

1925

Lewis publishes *Arrowsmith*.

1927

Lewis publishes *Elmer Gantry*.

1929

Lewis publishes *Dodsworth*.

1932

Huxley publishes *Brave New World*.

1945

Orwell publishes *Animal Farm*.

1949

Orwell publishes *Nineteen Eighty-Four*.

1950

Orwell dies.

1951

Lewis dies.

1952

Vonnegut publishes *Player Piano*.

1961

Heller publishes *Catch-22*.

1963

Huxley dies.

1969

Vonnegut publishes *Slaughterhouse-Five*.

1999

Heller dies.

For Further Research

Theories of Satire

Edward A. Bloom and Lillian D. Bloom, *Satire's Persuasive Voice*. Ithaca, NY: Cornell Press, 1979.

P.K. Elkin, *The Augustan Defence of Satire*. Oxford: Oxford University Press, 1973.

Robert C. Elliott, *The Power of Satire: Magic, Ritual, and Art*. Princeton, NJ: Princeton University Press, 1960.

Leonard Feinberg, *Introduction to Satire*. Ames: Iowa State University Press, 1967.

———, *The Satirist: His Temperament, Motivation, and Influence*. Ames: Iowa State University Press, 1963.

Gilbert Highet, *The Anatomy of Satire*. Princeton, NJ: Princeton University Press, 1962.

Matthew Hodgart, *Satire*. New York: McGraw-Hill, 1969.

H. James Jensen and Malvin R. Zirker Jr., eds., *The Satirist's Art*. Bloomington: Indiana University Press, 1972.

Alvin B. Kernan, *The Plot of Satire*. New Haven, CT: Yale University Press, 1965.

Ronald A. Knox, *Essays in Satire*. London: Sheed and Ward, 1928.

Ronald Paulson, ed., *Satire: Modern Essays in Criticism*. Englewood Cliffs, NJ: Prentice-Hall, 1971.

Louis D. Rubin Jr., ed., *The Comic Imagination in American Literature*. New Brunswick, NJ: Rutgers University Press, 1973.

John David Russell and Ashley Brown, eds., *Satire, a Critical Anthology*. Cleveland: World Publishing, 1967.

Charles Sanders, *The Scope of Satire*. Glenview, IL: Scott, Foresman, 1971.

John Snyder, *Prospects of Power: Tragedy, Satire, the Essay, and the Theory of Genre*. Lexington: University Press of Kentucky, 1991.

David Worcester, *The Art of Satire*. New York: Russell and Russell, 1960.

ABOUT SATIRISTS

Raymond Macdonald Alden, *The Rise of Formal Satire in England Under the Classical Influence*. Hamden, CT: Archon Books, 1961.

Frederick L. Beaty, *Byron the Satirist*. DeKalb: Northern Illinois University Press, 1985.

Harold Bloom, ed., *Modern Critical Views: Sinclair Lewis*. New York: Chelsea House, 1987.

Lloyd W. Brown, *Bits of Ivory: Narrative Techniques in Jane Austen's Fiction*. Baton Rouge: Louisiana State University Press, 1973.

Louis J. Budd, ed., *Critical Essays on Mark Twain, 1910–1980*. Boston: G.K. Hall, 1983.

John Marshall Bullitt, *Jonathan Swift and the Anatomy of Satire: A Study of Satiric Technique*. Cambridge, MA: Harvard University Press, 1953.

John R. Clark and Anna Motto, eds., *Satire—That Blasted Art*. New York: Putnam, 1973.

Pascal Covici Jr., *Mark Twain's Humor: The Image of a World*. Dallas: Southern Methodist University Press, 1962.

Herbert John Davis, *Jonathan Swift: Essays on His Satire and Other Studies*. New York: Oxford University Press, 1964.

Denis Donoghue, ed., *Jonathan Swift: A Critical Anthology*. Harmondsworth, England: Penguin, 1971.

William Bragg Ewald, *The Masks of Jonathan Swift*. New York: Russell and Russell, 1954.

Peter Firchow, *Aldous Huxley: Satirist and Novelist*. Minneapolis: University of Minnesota Press, 1972.

Claude Moore Fuess, *Lord Byron as a Satirist in Verse*. New York: Russell and Russell, 1964.

Richard Giannone, *Vonnegut: A Preface to His Novels.* Port Washington, NY: Kennikat Press, 1977.

Brian Gibbons, *Jacobean City Comedy: A Study of Satiric Plays by Jonson, Marston, and Middleton.* Cambridge, MA: Harvard University Press, 1968.

Stephen Jay Greenblatt, *Three Modern Satirists: Waugh, Orwell, and Huxley.* New Haven, CT: Yale University Press, 1965.

Ernest Jackson Hall, *The Satirical Element in the American Novel.* New York: Haskell House, 1966.

William Webster Heath, ed., *Discussions of Jane Austen.* Boston: Heath, 1961.

Gilbert Highet, *Juvenal the Satirist.* Oxford: Clarendon Press, 1954.

Anthony Channell Hilfer, *The Revolt from the Village, 1915–1930.* Chapel Hill: University of North Carolina Press, 1969.

Frederick Kiley and Walter McDonald, eds., *A "Catch-22" Casebook.* New York: Thomas Y. Crowell, 1973.

Martin Light, comp., *The Merrill Studies in* Babbitt. Columbus, OH: Charles E. Merrill, 1971.

Jeffrey Meyers, *A Reader's Guide to George Orwell.* Totowa, NJ: Rowman and Allanheld, 1984.

David Nokes, *Raillery and Rage: A Study of Eighteenth Century Satire.* New York: St. Martin's, 1987.

R.S. Ridgway, *Voltaire and Sensibility.* Montreal: McGill-Queen's University Press, 1973.

Edward W. Rosenheim, *Swift and the Satirist's Art.* Chicago: University of Chicago Press, 1963.

Michael Seidel, *Satiric Inheritance: Rabelais to Sterne.* Princeton, NJ: Princeton University Press, 1979.

Hugh Walker, *English Satire and Satirists.* New York: Dutton, 1925.

Stephen Weisenburger, *Fables of Subversion: Satire and the American Novel, 1930–1980.* Athens: University of Georgia Press, 1995.

INDEX